Advance Praise for *W*̶ ̶ ̶ ̶ ̶*emoir*

"I knew Kenneth from his blog, but his backstory is heartwarming and hilarious!"

—Andy Cohen, host of Bravo's *Watch What Happens Live* and author of *Most Talkative*

"For those of us who are fans of his blog Kenneth in the (212), who have always wondered just how Kenneth M. Walsh got to the big city of New York to keep us informed and entertained, he has finally let us in on all his wonderful yesterdays with his memoir, *Wasn't Tomorrow Wonderful?* Kenneth is the least mousey person I've ever met, and now I know exactly why after reading this witty and insightful book. He's exuberantly talented."

— Kevin Sessums, author of *Mississippi Sissy*

"Doesn't matter if you are gay, straight, or from another planet, you must read Kenneth Walsh's spectacular new book. Like Kenneth, the book is witty, serious, and passionate. It is a remarkable story of his personal journey told with humor and brilliant writing. Always have been a fan of this articulate and kind writer, and reading this book made him a new hero to me."

— David Mixner, civil rights activist and author of *Stranger Among Friends*

"Kenneth is, and always has been, a unique voice in the cluttered world of blogging."

— John Aravosis, editor and founder of AMERICAblog

"Kenneth M. Walsh is smart and fun, and so is his book, *Wasn't Tomorrow Wonderful?* By turns hilarious, poignant, and suspenseful—the Thomas Roberts story had me on the edge of my seat!—Kenneth makes his Alice in Wonderland-esque spin through Manhattan a journey we're more than happy to take with him."

— Dennis Hensley, author of *Misadventures in the (213)* and *Screening Party*

wasn't tomorrow wonderful?

a memoir

KENNETH M. WALSH

a.k.a. kenneth in the (212)

MAGNUS
BOOKS

Printed in the United States of America

First Edition

Cover by Chad Townsend
Cover photo courtesy of Fredrich Cantor/Photodisc/Getty Images
Digital and Print Layout by www.formatting4U.com

Print ISBN 978-1-62601-055-0
Digital ISBN 978-1-62601-056-7

www.riverdaleavebooks.com
www.magnusbooks.com

Wasn't Tomorrow Wonderful? is a memoir. It reflects the author's recollection of his experiences. Certain names and identifying characteristics have been changed.

For my mom—and the whole fam damily

table of contents

a mouse is not a home

I blame it all on Buffy and Jody. If it weren't for them, I might have had a chance at some sort of a normal childhood. Instead, I spent from age six on preoccupied with moving to New York City.

How I envied those two. Not only were their parents dead, they got to live in a glamorous high-rise apartment building in Manhattan, far away from the tract houses of the Midwest, where every home and every life looked just like the one next door.

Apartment 27A, where the twins lived with their jet-setting Uncle Bill and their big sister, Cissy, was like nothing I had ever seen before. The modern furniture. The city views. The butler, Mr. French, at your disposal. All of this *and* a second bathroom. Sure, Buffy and Jody may have had to adjust a bit after losing their parents in that horrible plane crash. But that paled in comparison to what I went through on a daily basis: getting ready for school every morning in the bathroom right after my stepfather, brushing my teeth and combing my hair in a steamy fog of aftershave and farts.

And then there was that fun doorknob at Uncle Bill's, with the big metal circle around it. I wasn't sure what its purpose was, but I knew it was luxurious—and way fancier than anything where I lived in Madison Heights, Michigan. Let's be honest: You didn't have to be in the advanced reading group in Miss Young's first-grade class at Roosevelt Elementary to know a Park Avenue address had more cachet than Tawas Court. And you could be sure Buffy, Jody, and

1

Cissy—who were originally from neighboring Terre Haute, Indiana, before tragedy rescued them from their mundane existence—knew it, too.

All of this, and I would never have to "go outside and play" in the backyard again. All those mosquitoes and unnecessary—not to mention exhausting—games of tag and hide-and-seek, putting your life on the line each time you got on the neighbors' rickety aluminum swing set that never seemed to be put together quite right. "It's fine," my friend's dad would insist, sweating and clearly frustrated that he couldn't quite figure out where the assembly had gone wrong. "Come and get us if *something* happens."

I figured that if I lived in an apartment like Buffy and Jody did, I'd be exempt from anything along those lines. If there had to be outdoor activities, I was more than OK with having lemonade on a chaise longue out on Uncle Bill's sophisticated wraparound terrace. The closest I wanted to be to "green grass" was of the indoor-outdoor carpet variety.

Admittedly, Buffy and Jody were just characters on the 1960s sitcom *Family Affair*. But they were proof that there was another way of life, and it was all the proof this grade-schooler needed.

My toys felt the same way. Although my Fisher-Price Play Family People (later known as "Little People") lived in a big house in the suburbs, the mother—who was a cop loosely based on Angie Dickinson's Pepper from *Police Woman* and myself—kept a sweet pied-à-terre downtown, right above the barber shop and city jail in the Play Family Village. And don't think for a second my Big Jim action figure lived in some dumpy barracks. He was shacked up with one of my Barbies in my Tuesday Taylor Penthouse Apartment, complete with private elevator, rooftop hot tub, and spectacular city views.

As I grew up, I continued to plot my move to the Big Apple. *Family Affair* reruns gave way to Woody Allen movies (all those glamorous neurotics in those huge apartments!), *The Goodbye Girl* (even struggling creative types could do it!), and *Desperately Seeking Susan* (that's where New Wavers like me live!).

Yet despite my precocious desires, there was one persistent thing that concerned me about the move, even as I approached adulthood. It wasn't the daunting expense, as I knew I'd never consider moving without a landing a job first. And it wasn't the distance. In fact, the principal reason I wanted to move was to get away from the suburbs of Phoenix (where we moved when I was eleven). I had been traveling to visit old friends in my native Michigan as long as I could remember, so I figured I could always fly home to see my family once I was settled in Manhattan. Even the crime— something that worried my mom horribly when I first went to New York City with friends as a teenager in the 1980s— wasn't a deterrent. The danger of it all was probably part of the appeal. The closest we came to urban decay in the master-planned community where I grew up in the "Valley of the Sun" was when "Jeffrey," who turned out to be a neighbor's juvenile delinquent son, "broke into" our house one night (barefoot!) after my parents neglected to lock the front door and stole my stepfather's wallet off the wet bar. Sure, Jeffrey—as we still refer to him more than thirty years later, a one-name moniker, normally reserved for divas worshiped by gay men—scared the crap out of my mom, who had fallen asleep on the couch only to open her eyes to find a stranger staring down at her. Terrified, she put her head down and pretended to be asleep, then after he left, she locked the door and went crazy running up and down the hallways of the house screaming for my stepfather, Gary. I didn't even get to enjoy this "big city" moment: I slept through the whole thing. But even this violation ended up seeming pretty rinky-dink when my mom later spotted our intruder at the neighborhood Mobil station, jotted down his license plate number, had him arrested, then identified him in a police lineup. The end result of Jeffrey's crime spree? My mom was so freaked out that she went back to work, and the quality of our dinner meals diminished measurably. Fancy Kraft Dinner (with Mom's signature tuna sauce) was replaced with making my own instant Mug-O-Lunch macaroni and cheese. Thanks a lot, Jeffrey.

What did concern me about heading east was something my life in the suburbs had nicely shielded me from: rodents. I'd never even seen a mouse, but the mere idea of one—let alone encountering one in my *home*—was almost unbearable. (Even the game Mousetrap frightened me as a child.) While I couldn't imagine that Buffy and Jody had to deal with anything so vile, I had heard that no matter where you lived, rich or poor, mice were never far from any New York apartment. Even Jackie O(h my God)! Still, I figured Mr. French simply had a word with the pesky varmint, and that was that.

I'm pretty sure I inherited my fear of these unseen creatures from my mom, who had regaled/terrified my siblings and me with a well-told horror story of the time she came face-to-face with a "cat-sized" rat that jumped out of a kitchen drawer she had opened when she was living in my father's hometown of Pottsville, Pennsylvania, home of Yuengling beer and complimentary black lung disease. Although my mom hadn't exactly grown up in the lap of luxury, her childhood in Omaha, Nebraska, and Montgomery County, Maryland, didn't have Pottsville's dirt basements and abject poverty, so when the rat introduced himself, the twenty-year-old new mom didn't think twice about my infant brother Bill's well-being, opting instead for the fifty-yard-dash out the front door. (Can't say I blame her.)

When I finally made it to the East Coast in the early '90s, I landed in Washington first. I'd had enough of Los Angeles freeways—having spent too much time broken down on the side of them in my beat-up '83 VW convertible Rabbit, the "convertible" part being occasionally *converting* it to run properly—so I decided to move to the nation's capital, where both of my older brothers were living. While this wasn't quite

New York City, it was the first test of my "city living" abilities and, more important, my rodent-coping skills. Sure enough, my first apartment had a "problem," as the super explained it, with people leaving the door open in the basement laundry room and rats coming in from the alley. That was all I needed to hear, sparking the beginning of a decades-long love affair with drop-off (and street-level) laundry service. While I avoided any rodent showdowns in that basement, I quickly found out I couldn't avoid them everywhere. Once, while I was sitting on a curb outside a popular coffee place in Dupont Circle, a rat came out of nowhere and darted between my legs, prompting me to let out one of my signature '80s slasher flick girl screams. This simultaneously cleared out the entire patio packed with customers, as well as any remaining testosterone in my nutsack.

When I finally moved to New York in 1998, I was feeling pretty comfortable. By then I had Troy, a fearless sixteen-pound tomcat who had been waiting his whole life to do battle with rodents of any size, and people assured me that mice avoided apartments where they could smell felines. This proved to be 100 percent accurate ... for a while. The first five or six years I never saw a single mouse, even as a neighbor told me about actual rats finding their way into his place. (This news was so unsettling that I considered getting a backup cat.) The landlord blamed a hole in the wall behind my neighbor's stove, but I didn't even want to hear the details.

But then, a year or two later, my boyfriend, Michael, spotted a "tiny" mouse in the kitchen one evening. The mouse was so small, in fact, that Troy didn't even notice it at first. I never saw it, either—I was reading in the living room—but just hearing these words sent me bolting into the bedroom with the door locked. (Because if you know only one thing about mice, it's that they have a hard time picking locks.) But Troy eventually punched his time card, swatted it with his enormous paw, and then choked the life out of it so Michael could quietly dispose of it. I was shaken, but when Michael told me that it was so tiny he was able to flush it down the toilet, I decided it was just a fluke, a newborn that had wandered into Apartment 3RW, still too young to be afraid of cats.

Around this same time, Troy got very ill. We eventually found out he had a giant tumor in his stomach, so we were going through the heart-wrenching process of deciding when to put him down, weighing his quality of life versus my need for protection. Now, I can't say with certainty that this was Darwinism in action, but as Troy's health deteriorated, mice suddenly started showing up on a regular basis, leaving me feeling terrorized in my own home as I was losing my best furry friend. Were these pests somehow sensing that Troy was no longer the threat he once was? The only other explanation I could come up with was that there was some digging going on nearby, but I never saw evidence of any.

Then one night it happened—my greatest fear come to life. Michael was sleeping at his place when I noticed Troy going berserk, in hot pursuit of *something*. My critter might have had a terminal illness, but deep down he was still a natural-born killer. I was paralyzed with fear, so I just stayed in the kitchen waiting for the whole thing to be over, thinking he'd eventually kill the mouse and I could get someone to dispose of it for me. But Troy kept carrying it in his mouth then releasing it—a live game of "cat and mouse"—so the thing would immediately start running around again, like a monster in a horror film that just won't die. I was standing on a chair in the kitchen shrieking (flipping through the unabridged Embarrassing Cliché Handbook) while Troy chased the mighty mouse into my bedroom. And then, as quickly as it had started, a suddenly subdued Troy came back out into the kitchen and laid down—mouseless. And that's when panic set in. For eight years, I'd lived in that apartment and had zero mice. Zero mice and zero roaches, a New York City anomaly that had me believing my life was truly charmed. Now, in the previous twelve months, there had to have been at least a half-dozen mice, probably more, yet somehow it almost always happened when I was not around, and Michael would dispose of the evidence before I had to face it.

But here I was—and for the situation to not be fully resolved was quite literally too much for me to bear. My first instinct was to move out and never even come back for my things. There was no way I was going to sleep in that bedroom knowing there was a mouse in there … *somewhere.* Of course, I called poor Michael, who was exhausted from a day out on Long Island visiting his family, and made him come over to look for it. He ripped my bedroom apart—the sound effects were straight out of a skit on *The Carol Burnett Show*—but the culprit was nowhere to be found. At that point, Michael decided the varmint must have survived the attack and slipped back out through whatever hole it had come in through. Exhausted and needing to be up at 6 a.m. for work the next morning, he tried his best to calm me down. I eventually, and very reluctantly, let him go, although I was certain, having witnessed it all, that the mouse was still lurking in my bedroom somewhere. About a half hour later, I was trying to put the whole thing out of my mind—talking myself into believing Michael's explanation—when I went to put some clothes in my closet and discovered a stiff little dead carcass lying on its side next to the dirty-clothes basket. I let out a blood-curdling scream. I could feel myself blushing—I was actually embarrassed for myself—but I could not pull it together and went running outside. (Over a tiny mouse that was *dead.*) Feeling much safer on the crime-ridden streets of New York City, alone at 3:45 a.m., I called Michael, who, by this point, had to be up in just a few hours, with the latest news.

"Just find something and pick it up," he said, his patience understandably waning. "And be happy that you can sleep knowing that it's over."

Only it was anything but over. There was still no way I could stay in that apartment.

As I stumbled down Eighth Avenue hoping to find a friendly soul to come dispose of this cheese-obsessed intruder, Michael suddenly appeared in front of me. He then walked back to my apartment. He went upstairs. He removed the mouse. He went home. He never said a word.

I slept like a baby that night knowing that the scary mouse was gone ... and that I had moved to the right city, where I would find a guy willing to love me no matter how ridiculous I might be, and who recognized that sometimes even rodenticide is a family affair.

i'm from everywhere

How do you answer the question "Where are you from?" when you've lived in half a dozen places, some of them longer than in the place where you were born?

My boyfriend, Michael, always teases me about being "from everywhere." You see, he's from New York. He was born in New York. He grew up in New York. He lives in New York. Both his parents and all three of his siblings were born and raised in New York. It's pretty straightforward—even taking into account a year he spent in Miami Beach. (But don't *all* New Yorkers eventually move to Miami?)

With me, well, I guess where I'm from depends on who else is in the room.

You're from Detroit? So am I! I was born just outside, in Royal Oak, and lived in neighboring Madison Heights until I was nearly twelve. After my family left the Motor City, I went back every summer to visit friends until I graduated from college. (Needed to squeeze in a few extra trips to Boblo!) From Korvettes and Little Caesars to Vernors and Town Club pop, I'm a Michigander through and through. And I can add an apostrophe *s* to the end of proper nouns for no reason with the best of them. ("Who wants to go to Kmart's?")

You're from Phoenix? So am I! We moved to nearby Mesa just before my twelfth birthday, and I went to junior high, high school, and college there. From Dillard's and Broadway Southwest to Peter Piper Pizza and Wallace and Ladmo, I'm a Phoenician through and through. It's also where I've called "home" the last thirty years because my parents

9

and my sister still live there, along with my sister's husband and my niece and nephew.

You're from Southern California? So am I! Orange County? Sure. After college I crashed at a friend's apartment in Huntington Beach for a while and then lived even closer to the ocean for a year while working at the *Orange County Register*. From the Boom Boom Room and Newport Station to South Coast Plaza and Fashion Island, I'm an Orange County guy. More of a Los Angeles type? So am I! Orange County was as boring as Phoenix, so I moved to the Westside of Los Angeles for a year, living in an apartment on South Bundy Drive just a stone's throw from where Nicole Brown Simpson and Ronald Goldman met their fate. I also lived there during the L.A. riots, after the cops who beat Rodney King were acquitted of all charges. I chose an apartment on Bundy because I thought West Hollywood would seem "too gay," but it didn't take long for me to realize my decision was just queer. All that living in West Los Angeles instead of West Hollywood did was ensure I'd have to drink and drive every night, because my roommate and I were entirely too gay not to go out every night in West Hollywood. A 1920s bungalow in West Hollywood was the solution, on a tree-lined street between Santa Monica Boulevard and Melrose Avenue just off La Cienega. Where else could a twenty-three-year-old suburbanite end up involved with a tattooed muscle-bound model on a Harley Davidson?

Oh, but you're from San Diego? My roommate in Orange County and I used to head down there all the time to go bar-hopping at Flick's, Rich's, and the West Coast Production Company. I later spent even more time down the coast when my stepfather's work took my parents to Carlsbad, where they bought a house in the La Costa area, one of the most beautiful communities I've seen.

You're from Pottsville, Pennsylvania? I've never lived there, but that's where my dad was born and raised—and it's the town a whole portion of the Walsh clan still calls home.

My brother Bill was born there, too. And it's just obscure enough that if someone mentions it, of course I'm going to claim it as my own. Nothing but the dead and dying in that little town, but my grandfather made a name for himself as a boxer, boxing promoter, and a sports writer at the *Pottsville Republican,* so it's a source of great pride for Walshes around the region.

You're from Washington? Funny thing, Washington's my "other home"! My mother lived in Takoma Park, Maryland, in the late 1950s and attended high school in nearby Silver Spring at the Academy of the Holy Names. She met and married my father in the D.C. area, and her aunt and uncle—Dorothy and Ernie—lived in Silver Spring and later in Potomac. We used to visit them a lot when I was a kid, going out to their little place in Rehoboth Beach in the summertime, before "the gays" took over, as Aunt Dorothy later explained it. When I was in college in the '80s, I interned on Capitol Hill and immediately felt at home in D.C.—then I moved there officially in 1993 and stayed five years. My brothers moved there as well. My oldest brother, Bill, and his clan are still there, and after returning to Phoenix for a number of years, my brother Terence is back in the Washington area, as are a big group of my closest friends (Ken, Jean, Kandy, Kristen, Paula). For many years after I arrived in New York, Washington was the go-to location for holidays when I couldn't be with my family in Arizona.

Oh, but *you're* from Virginia? I'm actually a former Virginian, too! I wasn't going to bring it up, but I did live in Arlington for a number of years with my Colombian boyfriend, Rafael. While many people think Northern Virginia is the same thing as living in Washington, it's really not. I can talk the Metro Orange Line and Rio Grande Mexican food with the best of them, and I got to know the countryside pretty well too, even though I wanted to live in the District.

So the next time somebody asks me where I'm "from" and I can't give them a straight answer, would someone please tell my guy to leave me alone? I think of myself as a New Yorker now—and I've heard it said that once you've lived here ten years, you become one—but if I dare tell people I'm *from* New York, Michael scoffs at a non-native claiming such rights. So until I figure out a better response, I guess it's true: I'm from everywhere.

blue gremlin

Around newsrooms where I have worked they're known as "Kenneth stories." If someone has been murdered, molested, or victimized in some horrible way, I'm the go-to editor. You'd think people would be a little creeped out by someone who "likes" to read about these things, but most colleagues seem to accept that I possess nothing more than a hyperactive sense of morbid curiosity, so they seem to find my interest in the criminal mind more amusing than anything else.

Lucky for me, one of my favorite coworkers, Mike, was a fellow crime junkie. We could talk for hours on end about unsolved mysteries, serial killers, and infamous murder cases. When the movie *Zodiac* came out a few years ago, Mike and I got going again when he told me he'd seen a rerun of Stone Phillips's prison interview with Jeffrey Dahmer from back in the day. Later he asked me if I was familiar with the Leopold and Loeb case. He described how when he was quite young he became completely intrigued with the tale of Nathan Leopold, Jr., and Richard Loeb, the lovers who kidnapped and murdered a fourteen-year-old boy in the early 1920s ... for "kicks." (I had actually heard of a movie about these men called *Swoon,* but didn't realize it was a true story.) Later, Jack the Ripper interested him, and he never looked back.

Then he asked me if I had any idea where *my fascination* came from.

Indeed, I did, I explained:

It all started the day I arrived as a transfer student at

Hiller Elementary. My mom had recently remarried, and the newlyweds decided a new house was fitting for a new start. So we moved during the middle of my first-grade year. Mrs. Lewandowski introduced me to the class as Kenny Walsh from Roosevelt Elementary, then suggested I sit in a recently vacated desk next to Mark Perrin.

"Hi, Paula!" was the first thing Mark said to me, although I could barely understand him because he was so tickled with his clever dig that he could barely get the words out. As the entire classroom erupted in laughter ("Settle down, kids," Mrs. Lewandowski scolded), I realized that my new desk had been decorated—complete with flowery decals and bubble lettering—by its previous occupant, who like every other girl born in the late '60s was named Paula, and who loved to see her name in writing. (OK, so she and I did have *one thing* in common.)

And just like that, my fate was sealed. If being a midyear transfer student didn't already make me the odd kid out, having the most popular (and dare I say cutest) boy in class decide you were "a girl" certainly did.

While the guys all turned on me, the girls were more accepting. My ability to do "hot peppers" on the playground made me a star on the jump rope circuit, so I tried to make the most of my menagerie of girl friends while I anxiously tried to figure out a way to win over the boys, a task that wouldn't have even been necessary if only my new desk had been previously occupied by a Blake or an Austin.

Life in the leafy suburbs of Detroit took an ominous turn around a year later when a twelve-year-old boy from nearby Ferndale was abducted, sexually assaulted, and murdered in February 1976. Prior to this, the worst thing to ever happen in sleepy Oakland County that I knew of was my failure to place in the Laura Ingalls Wilder diorama competition at Hiller Elementary. I had nearly killed myself fashioning the Ingalls family's farmhouse out of an old box from Kinney Shoes, and merely received an Honorable Mention, which I came to realize they gave to everyone who entered. But suddenly it seemed as if we had a much more serious problem on our hands.

Over the next twelve months, three more children were brutally slain, and panic swept the area as we began to come to terms with the fact that there was a serial child killer on the loose.

Known rather uncreatively as the Oakland County Child Killer—and sometimes the Oakland County Child Molester, although his sexual abuse paled in comparison to his murderous ways—this psychopath had all of Hiller Elementary living in terror, as he somehow managed to lure kids into his grip, seemingly in broad daylight in crowded parts of town.

Was he a clergyman? A police officer? Some other trusted member of the community? Everyone wondered how he could possibly abduct so many children—four confirmed and four others suspected—without anyone noticing. Each week, we'd have a new Don't Go With Strangers seminar at school—a motto I would come to routinely disobey as a gay man in dark singles bars years later. The lectures were accompanied by filmstrips, badges, handouts, and coloring books, proffering all the latest techniques for avoiding kidnap, rape, and murder.

While most of the kids at my school trembled at the mere mention of the subject, I found myself curiously intrigued, often engaging my teachers in lengthy discussions about the case, dissecting the scant evidence, and offering various theories. I also watched in awe that summer as New York City was gripped in fear as the Son of Sam began executing couples in lovers' lanes. But not a lot happened in my neighborhood, so a real-life serial killer roaming the streets of Oakland County was just the kind of excitement I was longing for. Truth be told, the whole thing felt more like watching a scary movie than something to be really afraid of, and I was well on my way to becoming a full-fledged horror-movie buff and true-crime fanatic, as demonstrated by the *Jaws* poster and Patty Hearst photo I kept tacked to my bedroom wall.

It didn't help to calm my already-wild imagination that the killer reportedly drove a blue AMC Gremlin with a white hockey stripe—*exactly* like my second-grade teacher's car. In fact, Miss Blackburn was kind of manly: What else might she be hiding?

I would religiously cut out all the articles from the *Oakland Tribune* and the *Detroit Free Press,* and study the profiles of the killer's victims, kids whose lives appeared to be similar to my own. Even while recalling the story to a coworker recently, more than thirty years later, I could readily cite the names of all the children—Timothy King, Kristine Mihelich, Jill Robinson, and Mark Stebbins. Each of them seemed like the kind of kids who could have been my friends.

Adding another creepy element to the already terrifying case was that the Oakland County Child Killer was known for meticulously "caring" for his victims, whom the police believed were alive with their abductor for several days, and sometimes weeks, before the gruesome end, which included strangulation, smothering, and a gunshot to the face.

Timothy King's mom went on television and mentioned that she looked forward to his safe return so she could serve him his favorite dinner, Kentucky Fried Chicken; the medical examiner later determined that Timmy had fried chicken in his stomach at the time of his death. The Oakland County Child Killer's victims were always bathed and had manicured fingernails and were wearing freshly washed and pressed clothing. For this reason he was sometimes called "The Babysitter" by the media. Having cared for children in my early teens, though, I think this name seemed rather odd, as I doubt killing the children—however tempting—would have been acceptable to anyone, even in those days.

So while all the *normal* kids were busy being afraid of the killer—the mere sight of a blue Gremlin driving past the playground sent them running and screaming in a panic—I spent a huge part of my time fantasizing that he would abduct me.

If being kidnapped by a child rapist and serial killer seems like an odd desire for a nine-year-old boy—did I have something against simply joining the Cub Scouts, you might be wondering—there was (what seemed like) a logical explanation at the time: It would make the other kids like and respect me.

So rather than dreaming of becoming a celebrated athlete, rock star, or some other kid-tested idol, my "I'll show you" fantasy centered around capturing my peers' boogeyman, and thus ensuring heroic status at least through sixth-grade graduation.

Having seen Linda Blair's tour de force performance in the classic made-for-television movie *Sweet Hostage* a couple of years earlier, I knew that the best way to deal with a deranged kidnapper was to befriend him. Admittedly she fucked her way into the good graces of her abductor, played by a young and dreamy Martin Sheen (clad in wife-beater and jeans), but I was willing to do anything for the cause, and I was already becoming aware that Mark Perrin might have been on to something with the way he labeled me that first day, although I couldn't quite figure out what. (Why did I get butterflies in my stomach whenever the elastic band on the other boys' Fruit of the Loom briefs became exposed when they were horsing around on the playground?) Once I had the Oakland County Child Killer's trust, I would be shrewd and clever enough to escape and then quickly race to the authorities to get him arrested, putting an end to that monster's reign of terror.

I couldn't wait to be on the evening news—or maybe even *Good Morning America* with Nancy Dussault and David Hartman! I would be lauded as a hero and finally be adored by my detractors, sometimes referred to as my classmates. I used to practice what I'd say during interviews directly into my mom's Goody hairbrush, giving answers that made me seem brave but never cocky.

"Why did you do it, Kenny?"

17

"It was just something I felt I had to do."

"Were you scared at all, Kenny?"

"I was only scared that this monster would remain free to harm other children."

Once the initial media firestorm died down, I figured I'd grant an exclusive sit-down interview to *60 Minutes,* perhaps with Charles Kuralt.

Despite my hours of meticulous planning, there was one thing standing between me and my destiny. Although the killer was definitely in the area—striking Berkley, Troy, and Birmingham, three of Oakland County's toniest cities—he never ventured into the more downscale city of Madison Heights to find his victims. That further fueled my growing sense of inadequacy.

All of that changed one night in early 1977 when my mom and stepdad happened to ask me if I wanted to go to the movies with them. At first, when they said they were headed to see the remake of *King Kong,* I wasn't very excited. Even as a child I hated science fiction pictures. Later that year, I ditched my friends during the opening credits of *Star Wars* and slipped into *Annie Hall* in the auditorium across the hall, where I watched in awe at what I hoped was my future. I really couldn't see sitting through two hours of a fake gorilla when I could be home listening to Olivia Newton-John's new LP, *Making a Good Thing Better,* which included a stirring cover of "Don't Cry for Me, Argentina."

But when I heard my parents mention that they were seeing *King Kong* at the Berkley Theatre, a plan was instantly hatched in my youthful mind: The Berkley was on 12 Mile and Robina—just a few blocks from the 7-Eleven on 12 Mile and Oakshire where Kristine Mihelich had been abducted earlier that month. If the killer wouldn't come to me, I thought, I'd go to him.

"I'd love to go the movies!" I screamed from my upstairs bedroom, before quickly running into the bathroom to make sure I looked cute enough to abduct.

My stomach was in knots as we drove to the cinema in my stepdad's brand-new black Malibu Classic. The anticipation was nearly unbearable, and I was becoming light-headed from my mother's cigarette smoke and the overbearing smell of Gary's Wild Country cologne. Avon began selling his favorite scent in bottles shaped like chess pieces that year—Mom bought him the whole thirty-two-piece set—and it seemed my stepfather had splashed on an entire rook that night. As we approached the theater I quickly scoured the parking lot and adjoining streets looking for the killer's signature blue Gremlin, but saw nothing. Inside, before the show, I scanned the crowd looking for anyone suspicious. I was barely nine years old, but I felt like a mature twelve, and I knew what needed to be done.

During the film, I discreetly excused myself to use the bathroom—alone—in the hope that I would find him lurking around the joint just looking for an opportunity to make his move. Those other kids may not have known what was going on, but I did. And now it was time for him to pay for his crimes. Outside the auditorium, the bathroom and lobby were empty but for an usher or two. After surveying the lobby and out front one more time it became clear that getting abducted was not in the cards that night—or any other.

Instead, I watched the rest of the movie with my parents. It was awful, but it did spark my long-term love affair with Jessica Lange. (Three years later, I would notice her again in *How to Beat the High Cost of Living* with my new best friend, Mark. No, *not* Mark Perrin.)

By the end of 1977, the death toll stood at four children and four other likely victims. And by the time my family moved to Phoenix in early 1979, the killings had stopped and no arrest was ever made. This move occurred midway through sixth grade, and the whole "pick on the new kid" scenario repeated itself nearly verbatim. By then, though, I had less of a desire to win over my peers and more of an inclination to go on a child-killing spree of my own.

Over the years—pre-Internet—I would periodically try to check in on the case. While working in the morgue at the *Orange County Register* in the early '90s, I culled through microfilm and microfiche to see if there had been any developments.

It wasn't until the twenty-first century, however, that some progress was made. Investigators took a fresh look, at the urging of Timothy King's family.

Eyebrows were raised when a convicted sex offender was offered a plea deal if he would take a polygraph about the Oakland County child murders, but he opted to accept full punishment instead. "I can't in my wildest dreams imagine why he wouldn't cooperate," the prosecutor was quoted as saying at the time.

Then in 2011, the *Detroit News* reported that Christopher Busch, who was the son of a prominent General Motors executive and was convicted four times of raping minors, and a companion, Gregory Greene, were considered two extremely viable suspects in the Oakland County child killings. Busch, who had passed a polygraph at the time, committed suicide in November 1978, and no OCKK murders happened after that. Greene died of a heart attack in prison in 1995 when he was forty-five.

This theory was bolstered later that year when the first DNA evidence of any kind was announced. It linked James Vincent Gunnels, himself a sexual victim of Christopher Busch's, to one of the murder victims. Police said they believed Gunnels might have been used to lure some of the OCCK victims. The DNA material that matched Gunnels was found on Timothy King. Fueling the suspicions, photos of Busch's bedroom, taken after his suicide, showed a drawing on the wall of a young boy screaming. The boy looks hauntingly like Mark Stebbins.

Despite the recent developments in the case—including the shocking discovery in 2013 of a blue Gremlin buried in the ground about fifty miles north of where the murders took place—no one has ever been brought to justice for the heinous crimes that brought my childhood neighborhood to its knees.

More than thirty years since the last murder, I often think about Mark Stebbins, Jill Robinson, Kristine Mihelich, and Timothy King. I also think about their families and how they never got the closure of knowing that their loved ones' killer was made to pay for his crimes. Although I know it's ridiculous, I even feel a twinge of guilt that I wasn't able to help them. Rarely, however, do I think much about Mark Perrin, and how he and his Hiller Elementary minions tormented me. Still, every time I read about the abduction of a child somewhere, I suddenly become "Paula" again, momentarily obsessed with what's going on and wishing I could somehow make things better. While I've never actually been able to solve any of the "Kenneth stories" I've edited or followed over the past three decades, somehow it makes me feel better to know that I once truly tried.

hooray for mollywood

"I don't get it."

That's how my mother first summed up her feelings about the world's cultural and financial hub, and how I first found out that if I was ever going to move to New York City, I was going to have to do it without her blessing.

"What's there that he wants to see?" she incredulously asked my brother Bill, as my friends and I planned our first trip to the Big Apple as teenagers. The year was 1985 and we were looking at hotels in Midtown Manhattan. But based on her reaction, you'd have sworn we had just giddily traipsed in the front door from the travel agency with applications for a visa to Lebanon.

In fairness, my mom is of the generation that prides itself on *not* having to live in the city, so despite New York's rather lofty reputation, it still managed to escape her why anyone would choose to go there on purpose. Still, her reaction sort of surprised me. Because growing up, I always knew my mom was different, in a good way, and I thought she would embrace my against-the-grain nature.

While all of my friends' moms seemed so old and matronly, doing "old-fashioned" things like asking about their kids' homework and driving them to softball practice, my mom was tall and thin and pretty, like Geena Davis if she had ever been in an advertisement for Silva Thin Menthols, Molly's signature cigarette. Rather than the usual suburban mom pursuits of getting fat and going to the salon to get "no-frills" hairdos, Mom loved to laugh, hanging out with her girlfriends who found her fun personality and sharp tongue to

23

be utterly magnetic, not to mention hilarious. All of my friends worshiped Molly too—as did I—even if we were all slightly fearful of what might come out of her mouth next.

Having been raised by a sadistic and mentally disturbed single mother in the 1940s and '50s, Mom occasionally seemed to lack certain basic parenting skills, most notably anything remotely resembling patience and tolerance, two things she certainly was not afforded in her own tumultuous childhood. Despite the protestations of many, her twisted mother—encouraged by the good folks at Catholic Charities USA—left my mom, her older sister, and her newborn half-brother in a church-run orphanage for four years when Mom was a small girl. Catholic Charities USA decided my grandmother was "gifted," so she would be better off going to college than being a mother. (Needless to say, the only thing gifted in this sad situation was the "gift" of a lifetime feeling of abandonment to her offspring.) Mom's younger half-brother, whose father my grandmother divorced during the pregnancy, spent a total of ten minutes of his infancy in the family home, in a basket on the washing machine, before it was time to go to the nuns. My grandmother eventually committed suicide at age fifty when her third marriage unraveled, and my mom had not spoken to her in the decade that preceded this event. The scars ran deep, but Mom did everything in her power to be nothing like her own mother.

Her love for babies was obvious. I saw it for myself when my little sister was born when I was seven, and again when my nephew and niece were born twenty-five years later. The way she smothered these completely dependent little creatures with love and affection was all-consuming, so I have no doubt she did the same with my brothers and me. Because of this, we all bonded with her deeply, a bond she says she felt with an aunt rather than with her own mother.

But as much as she loved babies, that sometimes seemed to be where her unconditional appreciation of children ended. The second you reached the age when you could have an opinion of your own, her patience would sometimes ran out. (I believe "mouthy" was how she described this stage in child development, which resulted in a fifteen-year "attitude" problem.) As an adult, I grew to have an endless amount of sympathy for her plight. She had her first baby when she was barely eighteen—a boy named Kevin who would live only two months—then my brother Bill came along a couple of years later. Terence and I followed, then my sister, Jennifer, was a bit of a surprise when Molly was the ripe old age of thirty-two. How anyone copes with one child—much less four—is something I will never comprehend. I'm sure this has a lot to do with my ardent support of Planned Parenthood, an organization whose services weren't available for a teenage girl looking for a way out of her abusive mother's house back in the late 1950s. But when I was a child, Mom's ambivalence was sometimes disconcerting—but frequently hilarious—even if looking back I know that I probably wouldn't have behaved much differently if I had been thrown into her position.

The truth is Mom got really lucky. Although she was ill-equipped to be a parent—she basically didn't have any parents of her own, my dad was an alcoholic whom she divorced when I was four, and my stepfather was a kid himself when he married into our family of four—each of her children was a stellar student and model child. All of this, even though there was virtually no academic oversight or encouragement in our household. No one ever asked what was going on at school—that was *your* business. It was just assumed that you would be smarter than everyone else and not embarrass her, and we usually did not disappoint. In fact, so unusual was our mature behavior that my stepfather's cousin, whose children were insufferable terrors in Mom's eyes—aka typical kids—once asked my brothers and me if our mother "beat" us before we went to family gatherings to keep us in line, as she simply could not believe children could behave as well as we did without the threat of bodily harm. And once Mom went back to work, she had more important things to do than track our every move, like smoking and making fun of her annoying new coworkers ... or whoever else got in her way.

Despite Mom's unconventional parenting skills—I would say she was "hands-off," but the truth is she did once make the effort of grounding my sister from going to church with a friend when she was in junior high school, so clearly she had her parental moments—I started out as the quintessential mama's boy.

I was so attached to her, in fact, that when she started dating again when I was a tyke, she used to have to put on her work uniform, a baby blue polyester dress that all the cashiers at Kroger sported, in order to leave the house at night. It was the only way I would "allow" her to leave. I would cry and become inconsolable otherwise, but even at age five I understood the concept of working for a living.

When she wasn't at work, we would have so much fun listening to Mom's records in her bedroom while my older brothers were at school, dancing in front of her full-length mirror—with my feet on top of hers—to Cher's "Gypsys, Tramps, and Thieves," "Backstabbers" by the O'Jays, or whatever else came up on her cool new K-Tel album, *Believe in Music: 22 Original Hits/Original Stars.* Later, she would openly, and without hesitation, tell my brothers and stepfather—whom she married when I was six—that I was her favorite. "He's the only one who's nice to me," she explained, as she fixed us bowls of my favorite "cereal": milk over broken cinnamon graham crackers.

Mom used to brag to her friends when I was in grade school about what a "good husband" I was going to make some woman one day, what with my unusual sensitivity, my love of conversation, and my ability to wax a mean kitchen floor. I surprised her once in grade school by putting the wax *over* the dirt.

Meanwhile, I was the proudest kid at Hiller Elementary when she signed up to be the "room mother" for my second-grade class. Everyone was so jealous at how young and cool my mom was. They called her "Mrs. C," although it was less a nod to Marion Ross's character of the day's most popular show, *Happy Days,* than an acknowledgment that they were too stupid to pronounce her new married name, which had three whole syllables.

After years and years of Most Favored Child status, everything seemed to change one evening when I was thirteen—the height of the aforementioned "mouthy" phase. I had my own life by then and my own friends, and my adolescence was in full bloom. I was walking past the bathroom in our house on West Kiva when I heard the sound of my little sister crying. I wasn't sure what was going on, so I paused for a moment to try to figure out what was causing her such distress. The door was slightly ajar, and I could hear the bathroom sink running.

"Hold still," I heard my mom say, clearly agitated that her six-year-old daughter was squirming around too much as, I came to realize, she was trying to wash Jennifer's often-tangled hair.

"Mom, no!" my sister cried again, as I heard what sounded like her head bumping against the faucet.

Concerned, I stuck my head in and quietly said, "Mom, take it easy. You're hurting her."

My mother, not expecting an audience, slowly looked over her shoulder and shot back at me in her news-anchor-perfect, Great Plains–accented voice, "Stay out of this, *woman.*"

This mortifying trip down memory lane never fails to amuse my friends: It elicits an irresistible combination of horror, delight, and uproarious laughter. It doesn't matter that they've heard the story a dozen times before—at their insistence, mind you, not mine. My friends always want me to back up to the second I started down the hallway, and they demand the full build-up to the vicious dismissal. And I never disappointed.

You might wonder what kind of person would say such a cruel thing to her sexually confused teenage son. The answer, surprisingly enough, is someone I would want to be best friends with—that's who!—thus laying the groundwork for my somewhat unconventional relationship with my mom. (She was kind of right: I *was* being a bit of a Mrs. Kravitz.)

Sure, my siblings and I have many happy "traditional" memories of Mom. Her delicious Thanksgiving dinners (baked yams and apricots), her ready smile, and her utter joy in spoiling us every Christmas. (She once ventured down to the dingy punk record store in nearby Tempe in the early '80s and surprised me with a promotional light box she found for my favorite singer Debbie Harry's new album, *Koo Koo*, that featured the Blondie singer with large arrows through her skull.)

But many of our favorite memories of Mom tend to be more like her greatest "hits." It was as if my mother were an ahead-of-her-time stand-up comedian—in-house and strictly downtown—shocking the world, or at least the neighborhood, one one-liner at a time. She was truly a riot to be around—a maternal cross between a drag queen and a caricaturist, with an uncanny gift for homing in on the thing someone was most insecure about, or saying the thing everyone was thinking but was holding in. If you were occasionally on the receiving end of one of her digs, it was well worth it, because she provided high entertainment in an otherwise dull suburban setting. And restaurants were often Mom's best venues.

One afternoon during summer break, she took Terence, Jennifer, and me to a local Coco's for lunch. My seven-year-old sister—whose biggest infraction to date was spending an entire summer looking adorable in a Wonder Woman bathing suit—made the callous decision to act like a seven-year-old. Naturally, no one can recall what it is that Jenn did that was so awful as to make our mother come unglued, but eventually Mom propped her menu up on the table to separate herself from her *enfant terrible.* Terence and I looked on in disbelief, half cracking up at our mother's sense of drama, and half mortified at the scene playing out before us. (It would have been a certain viral video in the twenty-first century.)

After the pimply faced kid came to take our order, he

reached to clear the menus from the table when my mom abruptly—and firmly—gripped the menu to stop him from taking hers.

"Leave it there," she snarled. "I don't even want to *look* at her."

The boy's look of utter horror—and the fact that a relief server was sent in to finish the meal—tells me some therapist has made a bundle off of that one.

Another night when I was in ninth or tenth grade, my entire family made a trip to Pizza Hut for dinner, a place we rarely went to because my stepfather, Gary, felt it was "too expensive." After Gary ordered the large pizza, the kid working there gleefully informed my parents that they were having a special, and all you had to do was create your own "coupon" by writing "MAKE IT A LARGE, MEDIUM CHARGE" on a piece of paper. My tightwad stepfather looked like he'd just won the Mega Millions jackpot, then turned toward my mom, knowing she likely had paper and a pen in her purse. Mom has little tolerance for games, so I was not the least bit surprised when she recoiled, sighed, then said to the guy, "Can't you just charge us for a medium?" her head shaking in a way that clearly said, "This is the stupidest fucking thing I have ever seen in my life." The kid laughed nervously—I'm willing to guess this hadn't happened before—then said that he needed the "coupon" for his paperwork at the end of the night. At this point my mom had had enough, and said with a sigh, "Just charge us for a large," as my stepfather looked on crestfallen about the 73 cents that could have still been his. (She was completely right. To this day, I won't use a coupon—even if my life depends on it.)

Then there was the Olive Garden incident, which my brother Terence still ranks as Mom's finest hour because she briefly turned into Emily Hartley on *The Bob Newhart Show*. This unreasonably chipper waiter came flitting over to our table one night, and introduced himself as Greg. He then began rattling off the specials, demanding to know if anyone wanted to try one of Olive Garden's "scrumptious" appetizers—"such as the Artichoke and Spinach dip or the Bruschetta al Pomodoro"—or if he could get us started with a glass of wine or a soft drink, to which my mom finally cut him off by saying, "Get the bread, Greg."

Of course, Terence might just as readily tell you about how Mom had the audacity to get mad at *him* for putting his arms up in self-defense when she'd try to smack him when he talked back to her. "You're hurting *me!*" she'd complain, as she'd sic our stepfather, Gary, on us to do the dirty work she no longer could.

A few years later, I was extremely ill and had been violently coughing for over a week. AIDS was all over the news by this time, so I was convinced I had pneumocystis pneumonia because I had finally fooled around with my first guy that fall. (I'd have been more scared if Aiden Quinn hadn't been so hot in the made-for-TV movie *An Early Frost*.) And if it wasn't AIDS, I was sure I at least had "ARC" (the pre-AIDS condition then known as AIDS Related Complications), yet my mom wasn't so convinced.

"You're *making yourself* cough," was her diagnosis, as she took a sip of her sun tea and then a drag off her cigarette, eye roll in bloom, irritated that my hacking was interfering with her "stories" on TV. A week later, I finally took myself to the doctor, who diagnosed me with "acute bronchitis."

After picking up my antibiotics, I informed my mom that the doctor told me that I had come just in time, that walking pneumonia would have likely been next if I hadn't gotten treated. Clearly overcome with remorse, she replied, "Now you're just being dramatic."

My sister—who was my mom and Gary's only child together—proved to be my parents' biggest nightmare, throwing them off completely by being the first remotely normal child. Bill and Terence were bookish, introverted types, and I was an under-the-radar closet case who rarely went far from home, other than the occasional concert or tennis tournament. So when Jennifer actually went on dates and to proms and acted like a real teenager—sneaking out her bedroom window once—my parents were ready to ship her off to boarding school, or would have been if my stepfather hadn't been so cheap.

"Just you wait and see, Gary," my mom ranted throughout my sister's adolescence, "your daughter's going to get knocked up by some Mexican."

My sister, of course, turned out just fine. Today, she and her Mexican-American husband are the proud parents of two beautiful children, Molly and Gary's beloved—and only—grandkids, AJ and Ally.

Things weren't always a laughing matter, though. My brother Bill was home from the University of Arizona one evening, doing laundry. He was pressing some clothes on a table-top ironing board he had placed on the floor when my sister—about six or seven at the time—began screaming uncontrollably. My mother was instantly annoyed—she couldn't hear the television from her perch on the sectional with all the racket going on—so she sent Gary to make it stop. Gary came flying into the bedroom and grabbed Jennifer by the hair and pulled the screaming child out of the room. It was only then that my parents noticed she had a burn mark the shape of an iron on the back of her tiny leg. She had somehow accidentally sat *on the iron*, something I would have loved to have seen my parents explain at the emergency room.

"When in the hell would we have had time to *abuse* our daughter?" I could almost hear my mom indignantly asking the attending physician, as he considered calling the police. "*Knots Landing* was on."

When Jennifer got home, Mom and Gary were naturally consumed with guilt, and showered their little girl with ice cream and a stuffed bear. And then, as if to prove she was truly a member of our family, Jennifer innocently looked up from her Dairy Queen hot fudge sundae and asked, "Why couldn't this have happened to Terence?"

(I hadn't laughed that hard since the time Jenn was about four and spontaneously vomited on the kitchen floor after she

31

went to throw something in the trash can and she inadvertently put her hand in some warm vanilla pudding that was left on a discarded TV dinner tray. I can't even imagine what she thought she'd touched.)

As for her father, no one in our family got it worse than Gary. My long-suffering stepfather was a twenty-four-year-old grad student when he married my mother, a divorced thirty-one-year-old with three smart-mouthed young boys. (Gary was only thirteen years older than my brother Bill.) They met at Kroger, where my mom was a head cashier and Gary was a bagger, supporting himself through his undergraduate degree at Wayne State University, and later his MBA at the University of Detroit. In many ways, they were a perfect match. They both had abandonment issues. Gary's mother had died when he was young, and his father was distant and unsupportive. And they both wanted someone they could make a real home with. Although my mom was seven years his senior, she had spent her entire young adult life married with babies. Gary was like the guy she would have dated had she not taken up with my dad to get away from her mom. But while Gary was the right brain in the relationship— brilliant with numbers and a gifted painter—his frequent malapropisms were like catnip to my left-brained mother, who never missed an opportunity to pounce on one of his errors.

"Put the leftovers in a lock-sack bag," Gary said to my sister one night after dinner, stumbling over *Ziploc.*

Without missing a beat, my mom began to sing, at the top of her lungs, "Pack up your troubles in a lock-sack bag, and smile, smile, smile!"

And smile, smile, smile we did. All three of us boys were card-carrying members of the Future Copy Editors of America, and pointing out misspelled and misused words on signs and menus was one of our major sources of entertainment. Mom was equally intolerant of grammar mistakes, and poor Gary never stood a chance. This is the guy who announced that his elderly father had been diagnosed with "Old-Timer's disease," called Betty Crocker's Mug-O-Lunch "Chug-O-Lunch," and each February ordered my sister to do her "Valentimes." (Let's not even get into his insistence on calling a lawnmower a "grass cutter.")

If behavior like this seemed normal within the family unit and was amusing when I relayed it to my friends—they would beg for more!—I would learn later that it was far less entertaining for them in the flesh.

After my family moved from Detroit to Phoenix in the spring of 1979, my best friend from John Page Middle School, Mark, came out to spend the summer with us.

Mark and I had only met that previous fall during mandatory sixth-grade camp at Cedar Lake, where I spent a week pretending to bathe (and never going Number 2), got a bad case of "Cat Scratch Fever" courtesy of a sexy "older man" (an eighteen-year-old camp counselor with a guitar and a beginner's mustache who was a senior at Lamphere High), and did drag in a parody of an Underalls commercial—in pigtails!—for the big sendoff talent show. My leggy body looked flawless in the combination panties and hose. And my racy line pulled from the television spot—*'Cause they make me look like I'm not wearin' nothin'*—brought me my one and only standing ovation to date. But after Mark and I bonded over a mutual disdain for dodge ball—he was chubby and not athletic, I was a stick figure and didn't like the way that red rubber ball made my hands feel dry—a lifetime friendship was born. That we had both lost our fathers at a young age, his to cancer, mine to alcohol, also bonded us, even if we never dared to speak of it.

Mark always loved my "Molly stories," as they were known (although I never called her Molly to her face), and even when I was on the receiving end of one of her tirades, I still had to appreciate her caustic wit and complete lack of tolerance for anything—a trait I share with her today. What scientists studying the whole "nature vs. (lack of) nurture" debate would give for an hour alone with us.

The spring before Mark came to visit, he was getting quite an earful about the verbal beat downs my mom would deliver to various service people in Arizona: Our newly built house still had some rough edges, plus we were having a pool installed that summer, and nothing ever seemed to be up to my mom's standards. This was a sentiment everyone in our family could relate to, and my friend was particularly thrilled when he witnessed how my mom handled the woman from the company who had been sent out to the house because of nicks in the brand-new vinyl flooring in the kitchen.

"Listen, lady: You seem to be inordinately preoccupied with *how* the nicks got there," Mom explained to the nearly floored representative, as Mark and I looked on from our perch at the breakfast bar. "I don't care *how* they got there. I didn't spend thousands of dollars on a new kitchen floor for it to already look like it was ten years old. Just rip it out and replace it now—do you understand me?" As always, Mom was undeniably right. It was her technique that ruffled feathers.

That same summer, a prank caller asked my mom if she'd ever had an abortion.

"No, but I wish *your mother* had," she calmly replied, as she hung up the phone and returned to watching *Ryan's Hope.*

Still, as much as Mark loved my mom—this ringside seat was something he'd always dreamed of—even his eleven-year-old self knew something wasn't quite as it should be.

After a summer of watching her come unglued over the most minor of things—something that for the most part didn't even phase me or my siblings—Mark's cherubic face apparently could no longer hide his horror one afternoon, and Molly took notice.

"That's right, Mark! I'm a bitch! Now you know the truth—I'm a bitch!" she screamed an inch away from his stunned face after seeing his reaction to her ripping into me one evening. I don't even recall exactly what set her off, but I do know that in lieu of hobbies, the majority of her free time was spent accusing me of "hiding" her ashtrays.

Years later, Mark confessed to me that he slipped into the bathroom after she'd gone off on him that day and took a scalding hot shower in an attempt to conceal the tear stains on his face. As the hot water washed away his horror, he frantically tried to come up with an excuse to change his reservation and return home early, where he would be greeted at the gate by his adoring mother. Mark also told me he thought it was odd that my parents—even when I was very young and had been gone all summer—were never waiting for me at the airport when I returned home. In fact, they usually hadn't even left the house by the time I'd landed. "We'll be at the south curb in an hour, and we'll slow down and open the door and you jump in so we don't have to pay for parking" were the standard prearranged instructions they'd given me.

My best friend in Arizona, Greg, whom I met in a tennis tournament when we were in junior high school, felt similarly. After meeting my new pal one day after class, Molly quickly informed him that he bore a striking resemblance to Art Garfunkel, music to the ears of every insecure twelve-year-old boy. Little did he realize this was much more flattering than what she had to say about him when he wasn't around: She proclaimed at the dinner table that night that Greg was about the "gayest person" she had ever met in her life. I was thirteen and my sister was six.

"Did you hear *his voice*? He sounds just like Donnie, only *gayer!*" she announced. Donnie, of course, being her gay friend from the bank operations center where she now worked, with whom she occasionally carpooled. Greg was just an adolescent when he told me it made him uncomfortable to come over sometimes because there didn't seem to be a "normal boundary" between parent and child in our household, a conclusion that was undoubtedly reinforced after hearing that my brother Bill had once responded to our stepfather's complaint about the way he had done some yard work with a deadpanned "Suck me, Polack." Not only was my brother not disciplined; neither parent uttered even a mild reprimand.

35

Like most parent-child relationships, things got a little rocky in my adolescent years. My mom was happy at first when I started my own babysitting service. Kenny's Kid Kare—which I cleverly abbreviated as "KKK" in the ads I regularly ran in our community's newspaper, the *Ranchers' Roundup*—was a huge hit, even if the Cohens across the street mysteriously never opted to utilize my services. In addition to babysitting for kids myself, the KKK also had a roster of sitters (my friends) whom I placed with families for a small percentage of the hourly wage. Success came quickly, and Mom was impressed by my business acumen. But everything came to a halt one night when my employees and I became embroiled in a prank-call scandal that rocked Dobson Ranch. What started out as (or what I at least thought was) a rather ingenious prank-call setup—get every person we knew to repeatedly call the same home over and over to inquire about "the patio furniture for sale," as if their number had mistakenly been printed in an ad for such goods, and then the more they denied having placed an ad, the more aggressive we'd become with our offers ("Fine, play hard ball with me. Five hundred bucks, but that's my *final* offer!")—turned ugly when the woman whose house we kept calling got the police involved on a particularly busy night for the KKK. As fate would have it, the calls were traced that very night to phones at houses where four of my sitters were working. That led to the arrest of four of my mom's friends from the Bunco League the following day. The charge? Aggravated harassment.

Mom was surprisingly restrained when she confronted me about this. Facing your friends after your son nearly had them locked up couldn't have been fun, but given that she still laughs about the whole "patio furniture" bit, I think it's because deep down even she had to admit it was pretty brilliant. But at the time, she had recently gone back to work. And the already difficult time she had maintaining her composure was beginning to show more than a hint of wear and tear, what with a career, a husband, and four "mouthy" children to deal with.

All through elementary school and junior high, I was active in chorus, despite the fact that I've been assured by just about everyone who has ever come into contact with me that I cannot sing. I think the choir teachers just liked having cooperative boys in the chorus, and for better or worse, my deep voice added something to our sound. Mom was fairly game during elementary school; she was usually present for my performances, including the time I pretended to play the xylophone in the 1976 Christmas pageant. Mom didn't appreciate it when that kid Dominic all but stood in front of me on the risers, though—he was blocking her view of me— and suggested I give a good push if he did it again. But by junior high, sitting through another one of the Roadrunner Chorale's holiday performances was no longer high on her list of after-work activities, even the year I was inexplicably chosen to open the show with a Hanukkah song, along with Mike Murphy, whose mother actually was Jewish.

"Why do I always have to go to that fucking place?" I could hear my mom complaining to my stepfather before they were supposed to attend my latest performance. "Only the parents of the brats should have to go down there."

She had a point—I didn't want to spend any more time at school than absolutely necessary, either. Still, I dutifully delivered my lines, even if I wasn't sure what being "Jewish" meant:

Sing we now of Hanukkah. Happy, happy Hanukkah. Join us as we dance and sing: Shalom! Shalom!

By high school, things seemed to be going a little more smoothly at home until uncomfortable questions about my love life began popping up. The New Wave music scene was all the rage in the summer of 1983, so I hoped my spiky hair, ubiquitous concert T-shirts (Thompson Twins, R.E.M., B-52's, Missing Persons, Go-Go's) and orange Converse high-tops would make me the coolest kid on the block, rather than the object of rumors about my sexuality.

Apparently not.

While other kids were having elaborate sixteenth-birthday parties planned for them, I was cornered by my stepfather on the living-room sectional on my big day.

"Your mother and I want to know if you're some kind of *homosexual*?" he asked me, my mom nowhere in sight but obviously the architect of yet another uncomfortable scene.

Stunned and humiliated—I really didn't know what to call myself at that point, and I certainly wasn't prepared to have that conversation there, with him—I replied, almost truthfully, "Not that I know of."

But if he was going to accuse me of something that fabulous, he could have at least included a new white Volkswagen Cabriolet for my coming-out party.

Later that same summer, my mom re-enacted a scene out of an episode of *Three's Company* by picking up the phone extension midway through a sentence. After a lengthy love affair with Aussie girl-next-door Olivia Newton-John—that lasted from *If Not for You* all the way through to *Xanadu*—I'd recently fallen in love with another thirtysomething blonde bombshell, only this one was pure New York cool: Debbie Harry of Blondie. (Yet another reason why I felt compelled to move to New York.)

Everyone in school knew what a crazed fan I was, so when word got around to a fellow superfan at another school, we arranged through a mutual friend to speak on the phone. I'd never even met the guy (Louis lived on the opposite side of town, which in a sprawling city like Phoenix is about a hundred miles away), but he called one evening to swap information about our favorite singer when Chrissy—I mean my mom—picked up the phone at the exact moment that my new pal was saying: "Do you know what Hot Bods is?" (I didn't.) "It's a gay club on McDowell." What my mom didn't hear was my "friend" saying that he'd heard they were playing Debbie Harry's new single from the *Scarface* movie soundtrack, "Rush Rush," at this bar, so he was hoping it would gain momentum and hit the charts soon. That was the end of the story.

I was unaware of my mom's eavesdropping, so I was puzzled when she came up to me as I was walking out the door later that evening to go play tennis with my brother Bill and hugged me, and inexplicably said, "Just please be careful." Bill laughed hysterically in the car and told me about Mom's sleuthing. I wanted to crawl into a hole, increasingly confused about my feelings for other guys.

When I finally decided to come out officially to my mom—when I was in college, during Thanksgiving break in 1988—I kind of figured it would be a bit anticlimactic given my boyhood fascination with women's tennis, my "flaming" childhood friend, and my lifetime of not having girlfriends. (Not the mention her getting my stepfather to "pop the question" on my sixteenth birthday.)

Yet as I spilled the beans that my off-campus "roommate" and constant companion, Derek, was more than just a friend, she somehow managed to act surprised, as if she had never bought me a Growing-Up Skipper—you cranked Barbie's kid sister's arm and she sprouted tits!—the greatest gift ever, straight from *my* Christmas list. Perhaps the only "shocked" mom routine I believed less came from the mother of a friend who had told his mom he was "attracted" to Jim Palmer's Jockey underwear ads when he was eight, yet she still about fell over when he broke the news about his sexuality when he was in his twenties.

I was trying to be sympathetic and everything—I realized that having your child come out is never easy, no matter how many obvious clues there may have been—but I was going through my own turmoil, having just been asked for a "trial separation" by my then-boyfriend. So I was almost telling her I was gay in order to have someone to talk to about my problems.

Not a well-thought-out plan.

While she said all of the right things that afternoon— "You're still my son and I still love you"—Mom grew cold and distant in the months that followed, opting to pick fights with me over everything and nothing, and accusing me of "choosing" to be "this way." Our relationship hit an all-time low when I called the police on her after she'd stolen my phone and answering machine out of my bedroom. They were in "her" house, so they were actually "hers" she informed me. The cops kind of saw it differently, but they politely suggested that I might want to move out. (They got an idea of what I was dealing with when she literally tried to push them out the front door, demanding to know what they were doing "in her house.") After they left, Mom and I got the giggles about how out of hand we'd allowed things to become and made up, but it wasn't one of my proudest moments.

Still, when I graduated from college that December, my parents opted to skip my commencement ceremony—they went with my sister to visit our old neighbors who had moved to California—with my mom telling me that there would be so many people in attendance that I "wouldn't even realize they were there anyway."

Instead, a guy I met when I interned on Capitol Hill during my senior year flew in from Indiana, as well as my childhood best friend Mark and his roommate Doug—plus the runaway my sister had living in her closet. (Shala couldn't exactly go to California with my sister, so she kept my friends and me company back at the house.)

I was grateful to have these friends accompany me, but I was at a loss. It turned out to be my parents' loss, too. The legendary Pearl Bailey gave a beautiful speech, and she would pass away shortly thereafter.

A couple of months later, I mentioned how hurtful the graduation snub had been during a fight with my parents over my mishandling of money. (I was erratic in making payments to them on a car they had helped me buy; then I bounced a couple of checks, and because our accounts were linked, the bank—without my knowledge—had taken the money from my mom's account to cover my misdeeds.)

"I didn't see any point in going to the ceremony," she informed me. "All college has taught you is to be a more of an entitled brat than you already are."

That wasn't quite the apology I had been hoping for, so I responded in kind. I don't recall what I said exactly, but it infuriated my stepfather, who decided right there on the spot that he was repossessing my car. He literally wrestled the keys away from me, then marched out to the driveway to do something. The car was already parked at *his* house, so where was he trying to move it is anyone's guess.

About thirty minutes later, he reappeared, sweating profusely and short of breath. It turned out he couldn't figure out which key did what—a Pole stumped by German engineering, go figure—so he decided to employ a different tact, suddenly trying the "I'm your friend" routine as he asked me which key was for the ignition.

I told him to go fuck himself—if he was going to take my car away from me, then he could figure it out for himself—so he then tried to reason with me with a more general line of questioning:

"OK, OK, Kenny," he said, spittle flying from his mouth as he held the keys in front of my face, now aching to know which was the magic one. "Is it on this ring?"

They were both at the end of their ropes with me, yet I've never really understood what I had done that was so upsetting to either of them. I was far from perfect. But as was often the case, their reactions seemed incredibly out of proportion to the situation.

Space was obviously needed, and I was out of the house permanently within a couple of months. Things immediately got much better, as Gary reverted to his backseat role and my mom and I became closer.

Over the years, we've come a long way, with her embracing my long-term boyfriend as if he's one of her own and me feeling as if I'm her favorite again—most of the time.

With age, she has definitely softened. When I broached the topic of my upbringing about fifteen or twenty years ago, she quickly interrupted me by saying, "I'm just proud of myself for never *killing* any of you kids." But more recently, when a child-abuse case made national headlines, she was

41

circumspect, saying unchecked rage and children could be a dangerous combination, and that she had a lot of guilt about the missteps she'd made along the way. She then told me that after I came out of the closet, she had to mourn the death of who she thought I was, and how difficult that had been for her. Still, she told me how she couldn't love me any more than she does now. Then she bragged about how successful all of her children had become, and poked fun at herself by saying she couldn't help but wonder how much more successful we might have been had she known what she was doing. It was a touching moment for me, and something I had longed to hear. I assured her that I knew she'd done the best job she could, knowing what a difficult set of circumstances she had been dealt. I wouldn't trade moms with anyone.

The older she gets, the clearer it is to me that she is one of those people who has a hard exterior to cover a deeply sensitive inside. Given the abandonment she experienced as a child, it makes perfect sense. And I am definitely my mother's child. I've got an equally sharp tongue, yet we'll both cry at the smallest thing, which can make communication very difficult.

Still, when I reflect on my relationship with my mom—beyond the ups and downs, and beyond the hilarious one-liners—it's how much fun we've had over the years that really stays with me. From watching the Carter inauguration on TV together, when I happened to be home from school with chicken pox ("She's going be so *embarrassed* when she sees this one day" was her assessment of the new First Daughter, Amy, as she skipped all the way down Pennsylvania Avenue while her parents desperately tried to hold her hands), to listening to Gershwin tunes together while painting my bedroom when I was a teenager, to going through old family photos as an adult, there's nothing but love between us.

She's even begun to warm up to New York a bit. I had been living in the city for only a couple of months in the late '90s the first time she visited. My parents had a twelve-hour layover on their way home from St. Martin, so they decided to take a cab into the city from JFK to see me and my new digs. To mark the occasion, my two brothers came up from Washington, so we could all go out to dinner. After the initial shock of my tiny third-floor walk-up apartment began to wear off, the whole brood poured out onto Seventh Avenue, where my mom—with the Empire State Building to the north and the World Trade Center to the south, both in plain view—turned her head left, and then turned her head right, and declared, "New York: I don't get it." She stood there clueless as my brothers and I died laughing, because I had predicted she would repeat her exact quote from 1985! En route to dinner in the West Village, we stopped at a local Irish pub to kill some time before our dinner reservation when our conversation was interrupted by two gruff-looking men who were playing pool.

"Would you like to pick a few songs on the jukebox?" the bigger of the two said to us. "We paid for ten but only found a couple that we liked, so we thought you might want select a few."

My brother Bill—a fellow music junkie and control freak—and I were delighted by this random act of kindness. So we said thank you and then ran over to the jukebox and picked some tunes before rejoining the conversation with the parents.

"I just don't think I could live here," my stepfather said, an hour into his big city life and a second after the nicest thing a stranger had ever done for me in my entire life, adding: "People in New York are just so *rude*." Mom nodded in agreement.

I was too flabbergasted to even try to respond. Or to explain to them that all the shopkeepers in my neighborhood know me by name, while my parents' local businesses are manned by a revolving door of faceless teenagers. Not to mention that they live in a town halfway between Phoenix and Tucson, so far out in the middle of nowhere that if your car broke down, it would be inconceivable that you would *not* be raped and left for dead before the sun came up.

But on a more recent visit, after an afternoon at the American Museum of Natural History with the grandkids, followed by a glorious guided tour through Central Park, led by my native New Yorker lover, my mother began to see things differently.

As Mom and Michael strolled arm-in-arm through Poets' Walk, he pointed out the Carousel, the Zoo, the Essex House, and all the horses and carriages (known as hansom cabs) parked in the distance not far from the iconic Plaza Hotel.

"I think I finally get it," she told him with the excited smile of a little girl, as I was walking right behind, not wanting to miss a word.

And the truth of the matter was, I was feeling the exact same way about her.

death of a salesman

When I was growing up, my parents didn't believe in giving us an allowance. "You get to live here," was how my stepfather, Gary, explained the "allowance" we did get, which required that my siblings and I perform a litany of chores that included taking out the trash, cleaning the kitchen every night after dinner, and maintaining the swimming pool and hot tub, something other families hired professionals to do. Making iced tea was practically a full-time job in our house, too, but it wasn't even counted in the rotation of chores. Based on the lengths to which we would all go to avoid being the person to have the last glass, you'd think pouring two quarts of water and four scoops of powder into a green plastic pitcher (that had a built-in plunger to do the stirring) was more difficult than mowing the lawn on a 110-degree afternoon.

But as a kid with a lot of material needs, I needed cash—and lots of it. For starters, Mark, my best friend in Michigan, and I had made a pact when my family moved to Phoenix in 1979: We would visit each other every summer, taking turns being the host. Airfare wasn't cheap, so between saving up for that and my obsessive need to buy tennis equipment and record albums, this preadolescent had to get creative.

Being entrepreneurial was something that seemed to come naturally to me, or at least the part about separating people from their money. It started even before the move to Phoenix. After a series of successful Country Time lemonade stands—as a latch-key child, I didn't trust anything that wasn't processed and packaged, plus I found the profit margin was better with the powered mix and much easier to manage than all of those messy "natural" ingredients—my brothers and I set up a newsroom in the basement of our house in Madison Heights, and began to publish what we christened the *Hiller News*. We weren't going to let the fact that our crack school *didn't even have a newspaper* stop us—can you imagine a grammar school with no investigative reporters?—plus Scrabble tiles made for nifty name plaques. That we got permission to print the paper using one of the school's "ditto" machines—that used that strong-smelling purple ink—was a major score, and foreshadowed my future love of poppers. I was nine, and working at the *New York Times* was soon on my list of goals.

The paper didn't last long. Woodward and Bernstein had just brought down a president, and Principal Kwapisz wasn't about to let us do the same thing to him after Billy wrote a scathing op-ed blowing the lid off the lunch ladies not doing their job, which made the principal look bad. So Mr. Kwapisz shut us down after just a few issues, just as we were about to hire an advertising team—and possibly make some cash. But the seed had been planted, and I just kept coming up with new schemes. (But seriously, *were* the lunch ladies *afraid* of the students? And was the so-called "snowball area" only created to allow the kids to kill each other "peacefully" with snowballs and save supervisors the work of keeping them out of other trouble? To this day, no one has ever satisfactorily answered these questions.)

The following year, I was collecting quarters in exchange for advice (à la Lucy van Pelt) at my desk in Mr. Kamila's fifth-grade classroom. The kids would actually line up before and after class, so I had to get creative to meet their needs, with mini-sessions that were sort of a precursor to Lisa Kudrow's three-minute one-sided chats on *Web Therapy*.

"Don't worry," I assured one despondent student I wasn't able to "treat" one day during regular appointment times. "I'm going to extend my hours into midday recess." And I did, figuring out yet another way to avoid going outside to play.

Sure, I wasn't licensed. But at age ten, I was a burgeoning judgmental queen—and my tiny waist and straight-A average surely qualified me for something.

"You really don't know why Johnny won't go out with you?" I said to a mousy-looking classmate named Dara. "You've gotta do something about that hair. It's so greasy, it looks like there's an entire bottle of Tame creme rinse in it—that you forgot to rinse out." (I didn't even get started on those Garanimals and the extra fifteen she was carrying around.)

At twelve, I was charging admission for plays I was staging in my garage. These productions took place around the holidays. They were usually based on *Carol Burnett* skits I had memorized, and often involved me donning a long brown wig playing all of the female parts. With no money spent on production, fifty cents a kid really added up.

By thirteen, I had started my Kenny's Kid Kare babysitting service—this was back when parents would leave wooden spoons out on the countertop for you to discipline the children with, so babysitting was still fun—and I had so many clients that I began collecting additional fees for placing friends of mine into jobs I could not do myself.

Around the same time, my brother Terence and I started delivering our local newspaper. Because our neighborhood was brand new, the paper guaranteed a steady monthly "salary" regardless of how few subscribers you had.

"The *Mesa Tribune* will pay you the sum of forty dollars," was how it was put by the hillbilly of a woman who showed up at our house to conduct our initiation into the life of a paperboy. As she explained it, I would be paid as much as kids with a hundred houses for a route she was offering with just nineteen. (Perfect!) What she was never able to explain was why her tagalong daughter's name was "Margeny." We were told it was pronounced "MARG-in-ee," as if that somehow made it better.

Forty bucks a month sounded pretty enticing to a kid making a dollar an hour babysitting (the going rate at the time), but this "huge" amount didn't seem so great once I realized that it required working seven days a week for at least two hours a day, which amounted to an hourly wage of about seventy cents. And when you factored in the time you spent collecting—which sometimes meant begging people to give you the money they owed you—it was even less.

The only reason I didn't entirely despise this chore was that I found myself getting giddy whenever I'd go to collect at the house of a thirtyish bachelor who lived on the other side of Lindner Avenue in one of the ranch-styled houses from the American Continental model homes. I'd always set out to collect when I knew the man of the house would be home— the housewives always claimed to have no money, although I was usually asking for no more than a few bucks. This particular customer—medium height, with a lean muscular build and curly dark hair, reminded me of Gregory Harrison, if Gregory Harrison were, say, an insurance salesman in the suburbs of Phoenix. He would always be halfway out of his dress clothes by the time I would show up asking for money. He'd usually be on his back porch having a beer or watching TV on the sofa with his big feet in black socks up on the ottoman when he'd see it was me through the screen door and wave me in while he jumped up to grab his wallet or fumble through his change bowl I could hear rattling in the kitchen. His dress shirt would always be undone a few extra buttons, and his tie would often be loosened yet still around his neck. It's a look that still has a weakening effect on me.

Being gay was not something that registered in my young brain, but I do recall thinking it would be just fantastic if he mistook me for a girl and tried to kiss me … even once. This reverse *Just One of the Guys* scenario probably wouldn't have held up in a court of law—a thirty-year-old man kissing an eleven-year-old girl probably isn't any less illegal than a thirty-year-old man kissing an eleven-year-old boy—but I wasn't really thinking it through that far. The smell of his Brut aftershave was clouding my mind, as was the sight of his thick dark mustache. It never happened, but he helped keep my bookkeeping in excellent order.

It didn't take long before I realized the real way to make money was through sales. Each weekend, one of the newspaper's district managers would round up a bunch of paperboys and drive us to an untapped neighborhood to go door-to-door selling subscriptions.

In retrospect, this might not have been the safest thing to do. The whole child-abduction fad was really catching on— Etan Patz had been kidnapped that very May, and Adam Walsh was next—and we had already seen what the Oakland County Child Killer had done back in Detroit. But for whatever reason, no one seemed too concerned with the fact that we would inevitably end up alone in strangers' houses, pretty much begging to be the next kid featured on the side of a milk carton.

Even if no one got around to kidnapping you, though, you could be sure that by showing up unannounced at people's houses, you'd see some pretty messed-up stuff. My favorite was the time I interrupted a "slow dance" between a guy in his bathrobe and his inflatable "date"—a curvaceous blonde who appeared to be preemptively ready for a physician to examine her tonsils—in the middle of the afternoon. He wasn't nearly as hot as my Dream Customer, but I was offended that even *he* didn't try to molest me. Was I really that awkward a preteen?

Each "start," as they were known, would pay a buck, and every time you finished with the most starts in a weekend, you'd also get points toward fun prizes in a catalog. I'm not sure why, but I really excelled at this, almost always coming out on top and easily making enough money to pay for plane tickets, tennis rackets, and other luxuries.

I'd get to the prospective customer's house—each one looked the same except the driveway might be on the opposite side—and I'd turn on a character.

"Hello, sir. I'm with the *Mesa Tribune.* We're having a

great special to welcome new residents to the city. Do you like to read the evening paper?"

Straight white men—and in Mormon-heavy Mesa, that's pretty much all they were—loved to talk about themselves, so they'd immediately bite.

"Well, you know. I do like to check out the sports scores, and I do like to flip through ..."

Before I knew it, I had them eating out of my hands.

My parents, who normally didn't get overly involved in their kids' affairs, couldn't help but take notice of my success, and started to talk about what a big future they thought I had ahead of me as a "businessman" ... whatever that meant. But even then, I began to detest the whole act of selling because it was becoming apparent to me that I frequently had to fudge the truth to close the deal. We were always hawking subscriptions in neighborhoods where the paper was just setting up new routes and I wouldn't actually be the carrier. But the people would almost always agree to sign up because they liked the kid at the door, not because they liked the paper. (The "real" papers were the *Arizona Republic* and the *Phoenix Gazette,* so getting someone to take the *Tribune* was no easy task.)

"Will you be my paper ... *carrier?*" they would ask hesitantly, not entirely sure if I was a cute tomboy or ... what. The confusion was understandable. When I look back at photos from that era, the resemblance to Kristy McNichol is somewhat uncanny.

If they weren't enamored with the friendly shemale on the Huffy 10-speed—the Santa Fe model, which matched my hair and skin tone best—they would be signing up because they liked the idea of meeting their carrier upfront, so they could get a verbal guarantee that I would put the paper in a specific place. (Anal retention was alive and well even before I'd heard the term.) I'd usually just smile and not correct them: "Oh, yeah," my look would convey. "I can see why you would want the paper just behind the flower pot. Your neighbors do seem a bit untrustworthy." I knew it was wrong, but I'd play along because I wanted the money.

Feeling increasingly uncomfortable with my unethical business practices—and with delivering papers in the sweltering afternoon heat—I decided to go into business for myself. I had just entered junior high in the fall of 1979, and my obsession with office supplies—which continues to this day—had reached a fever pitch since I was busy writing several letters a week to my various friends back in Detroit. While other boys were spending countless hours at the Aladdin's Castle video game arcade at the local mall, pouring quarters into machines for games of *Asteroids* and *Space Invaders,* I spent my free time flipping through the pages of my mom's Lillian Vernon catalogs, hoping to buy enough stuff to qualify to receive the free "Mystery Grab Bag."

Not content with simply having a vast selection of stationery, I indulged in all of the accoutrements, like a fancy letter opener—which doubled as a murder weapon in the Super 8 mm slasher films I wrote and acted out around the house with my friend Mike (perfect for opening a letter from a good friend before killing a not-so-good one)—an envelope moistener (who could expect to come up with enough saliva to lick all those letters in that oppressive desert heat?), a vintage-looking postal box with a dozen cubby holes in which to file everything away, plus cool pens, stickers, and anything else that I could find on the pages of every teenage boy's favorite periodical: the Fingerhut catalog.

My classmates at Rhodes Junior High were intrigued.

"Where did you get those folders?" they would ask. Or, "Where did you get pencils with your initials on them?"

And this is where the idea of starting my own office-supply business was born. Because this happened before society had convinced me that as a homosexual I was defective, I exuded a naturalness and confidence that others found intoxicating, making me the Paper Clip Pied Piper. I couldn't see that, but I could see dollar signs.

Inspired by the famed Hanover House catalog—the Cadillac of mail-order crap—and with a tip of the hat to Wacky Packages, I christened my business Handitover House. Talk about an instant success! I'd order stuff in bulk from my mom's catalogs, then I'd stock up on other items from the local drugstore over in the Bashas' supermarket strip mall next to Peter Piper Pizza. Then I'd repackage everything with an obscene markup and watch the items fly off the shelf, from an office I'd set up in the loft—a small space created in the vaulted ceilings of our home that you reached via a spiral staircase—where I housed my considerable inventory. Given my new role as the ultimate "retailer," where markup is the name of the game, it became apparent my reservations about selling misleading newspaper subscriptions had more to do with my profit margin than my ethical makeup.

My label maker was a particularly wise investment, as kids would pay me to punch out labels for everything from their books to their records. (You never knew when another kid would show up with a copy of Olivia Newton-John's *Totally Hot,* and the fur would start flying over whose was whose.) When quarterly sales numbers began to go flat, I decided it was time to expand my customer base, targeting the women in the neighborhood. After school, my friend and neighbor Tammy—who we pretended was my cousin even though the lie wasn't funny and served no purpose whatsoever—would sometimes help me sell stuff door-to-door, with the real housewives of Dobson Ranch going gaga over the latest stationery I'd gotten or the newest gadget I'd found. A personalized stamp? Your own embosser? Have cash and hand it over, and it can all be yours!

The housewives adored me (the sweet boy with the bag full of pretty things), and Tammy (the athletic brunette with short hair who turned out not to be a lesbian, despite what her impressive collection of basketball trophies was saying about her behind her back) was not shy about asking for the cash.

My brother Terence still cringes in awe about the time

Tammy really had to lay down the law. I had just completed a sale with a dead ringer for Linda Lavin—three packs of stationery ("Those flowers are just *beautiful,*" she purred!), a moistener, and a box of ballpoint pens—when the woman mistakenly thought Tammy had neglected to give her change. As she pointed to money that was still in my helper's hands, Tammy snapped back, "Shut up, lady. It ain't your money!" in what can only be described now as an unorthodox "Good Salesman, Bad Salesman" technique. Money in my pocket, I smiled and we were on our way to the next house. Working under the radar of the Federal Trade Commission, we were very successful.

Never mind that the "personalized" stationery actually consisted of my brother Bill's "nice" handwriting on pieces of white paper with various colors of felt-tip pens. Handitover House lasted most of seventh and eighth grade. But by ninth, the freshman tennis team and adolescent drama had taken control of my young life, so I shut down the business. Still, my parents were crushed a couple of years later as I prepared for the Pre-ACT exam and I told them I wanted to major in journalism in college, not business. The experience of running the *Hiller News*—along with seeing Robert Redford in *All the President's Men* and a research paper I had done on the Pentagon Papers—had convinced me that a career in newspapers was for me and the *New York Times* was the place I wanted to be.

"But you would make such a great businessman," my distraught mom pleaded, not realizing that I was already flirting with the wrong side of the law and, if I were going to be crooked, I was probably better suited for politics.

She was so distraught, in fact, that I later listed "Hotel and Restaurant Management" as my likely major when I took the ACT exam, just to appease my parents, even though I was pretty sure you went to college to *avoid* winding up being a hotel or restaurant manager.

It really wasn't until I was in my late thirties that I

stopped hearing how successful I "might have been" if only I'd majored in business. "You were *soooo* good at sales when you were young," my mom would remind me, as if later actually landing my dream job as an editor at the *New York Times* meant I had not lived up to my potential. "You really could have been quite successful if you'd pursued business," she insisted, as I tried to tell her about attending my first Page 1 meeting at the famed Gray Lady, when Howell Raines was still editor in chief and a young reporter had just been caught plagiarizing and threatened to destroy the Paper of Record's reputation.

Of course, listening—especially on the phone—was never really her strong suit. Never mind a story about a new job. I could have been telling her about something far more incredible and she'd be just as likely to be distracted.

It would sound something like this:

Me: "So, Mom. I've got some wonderful news. I discovered a cure for cancer!"

Her: "Gary," hand covering the receiver to no avail, "what's burning?"

Me: "Mom, did you hear me? I discovered a cure for cancer."

Her: "Gary! Don't eat that cheese! It's for the lasagna! What now, Kenny?"

Mom's "business savvy" comments never really bothered me—I was kind of surprised she'd even noticed, and I know she just wanted what was best for me—but they did strike me as a bit odd. I mean, I ran around in Daisy Duke short shorts all through my youth with my nuts hanging out, yet my mom never encouraged me to be a male stripper. So I couldn't understand why my parents were so fixated on this particular talent I'd displayed early in life, yet never realized it was equally remarkable, or at least prophetic, that I'd started that school paper in fourth grade and then wound up with a successful career in media, as did both of my older brothers.

Of course, maybe my parents knew something we didn't.

The *Hiller News* took an extraordinary amount of time and effort to produce, but with no advertisers it was a money-losing proposition from the get-go. And all these years later, careers in journalism are collapsing, thanks to the Internet— with my dream job at the *New York Times* ending in devastating mass layoffs. Meanwhile, all those "businessmen" on Wall Street spend weekends away from their Park Avenue co-ops at their estates in the Hamptons while I plug away as a blogger in a tiny third-floor walk-up, relying on my childhood talent for being able to sell anything just to convince myself that I made the right call.

catch 'em doing good

The late '60s were a tumultuous time in America's history, and in recent years we've been marking big anniversaries of a number of events that shaped the nation: the Detroit riots, the assassinations of Bobby Kennedy and Martin Luther King, Jr., Woodstock.

Perhaps the event of that era that fascinated me the most happened during a forty-eight-hour period in 1969: the shockingly gruesome Tate/LaBianca murders, when members of the "Manson Family" slaughtered seven people, including the eight-and-a-half-months-pregnant movie star Sharon Tate. My self-diagnosis attributes my true-crime obsession to the blue Gremlin that still drives around inside my head, but the Manson crimes first captivated me in a most unlikely setting.

The year was 1979, and my family had recently moved from Detroit to Phoenix. I was the new kid at Rhodes Junior High School in suburban Mesa, Arizona, and while my classmates weren't quite sure what to make of me, my seventh-grade English teacher, Carol Carney, and I had immediately hit it off. (What twelve-year-old boy doesn't click best with middle-aged women?)

Mrs. Carney, a petite blonde with a pageboy haircut (picture Joyce Bullifant with a red pen), was the perfect teacher: sweet, friendly, and always with a word of encouragement. I don't recall where she said she was originally from, but it is now inconceivable to me that it wasn't Iowa. Every week, she would shower me with praise, always taking the time to send me home with congratulatory messages written on gold or maroon—our school colors—note cards emblazoned with the words "Catch 'Em Doing Good" on the front.

"Kenny got a ninety-eight percent on his grammar test this week!" "Kenny got an A on his essay this week!" "Kenny aced his spelling test this week! You should be very proud of him." By mid-semester, my bedroom was wallpapered in praise, as my reading teacher, Ms. Herman—an overweight Jewish lesbian with whom I also clicked—was also prone to catch me doing good.

When Mrs. Carney and I weren't laughing hysterically after class discussing the latest school gossip, we were busy dissecting the latest issues of *Family Circle* and *Ladies' Home Journal,* and discussing which contests we were going to enter from our mags. Mrs. Carney and I both *loved* contests.

Our relationship was taken to "the next level" one afternoon when she asked me if I'd be interested in babysitting for her. *Would I?* As if I wasn't secretly DYING to see what her house looked like, not to mention *Mr*. Carney. I felt as if Ed McMahon had just pulled up outside my English class.

I'd already said yes before I found out that Mrs. Carney's child was actually an infant. Although I was experienced with children—I was the genius behind Kenny's Kid Kare, after all—I had never so much as changed a diaper. In fact, I was pretty sure I'd gag if I ever had to. But at that point, there was no turning back; I'd have done *anything* for Mrs. Carney, a devotion that didn't go unnoticed by my mom.

Fortunately for everyone, when I arrived at the Carneys' house—a modest three-bedroom ranch, in case you're wondering, but on the *wrong* side of Alma School Road (what did I expect? She was a teacher, and her husband seemed kind of blue-collar)—the baby had already been put down for the night. After some awkward small talk in the kitchen—it always felt strange seeing your teacher out of context, even The Great Mrs. Carney—she and her husband took off for an evening on the town. Instantly bored with what was on television—neither *The Ropers* nor *Detective School* really held my interest that evening—I began scouring the bookshelves in the front room. It was pre e-books and pre-iTunes, so you could learn everything you needed to know about a person by the things in their house.

And then there it was: This giant black hardcover with creepy red lettering that all but jumped out at me ... *Helter Skelter*. That the dust jacket was frayed made it all the more creepy. I knew what it was about—Charles Manson, of course—but I was almost too terrified to open it. Still, as Mrs. Roper made one more joke about Stanley not putting out, the temptation was just too much, and I found myself just too sickly intrigued to even think of leaving it in its place. So I dug in, each page more terrifying than the one before. For the next three hours, every little creak in the house or sound from outside nearly sent me into a panic, ready to make a hasty escape. (That there was a defenseless baby in the other room never crossed my mind.)

I read nonstop that night until the Carneys got home. But, feeling I was doing something I shouldn't be doing, the second I saw the headlights in the driveway, I flew back to the bookshelf and put the book back where I'd found it, concerned that it wasn't in the exact slot as the neighboring books—*The World According to Garp, The Westing Game,* and a couple of Stephen Kings—had taken a tumble. Even though she was my English teacher, and she was impressed by my extensive reading list (much to my surprise, I was apparently the first seventh-grader she'd ever compared notes with on the latest Erma Bombeck), I was too ashamed or embarrassèd to let her see me reading *Helter Skelter,* let alone to ask to borrow it. Something about the boy babysitting your newborn daughter being *really into* the Manson murders just didn't seem likely to go over well. So as a workaround, I spent the next year or so eagerly returning to babysit just to get back to where I had left off in Vincent Bugliosi and Curt Gentry's masterpiece.

The day after my first babysitting job for Mrs. Carney, I was hanging out in my room after school when my mom came home. We'd gotten into a screaming match over nothing—something that became increasingly frequent once I became an adolescent and she went back to work—when she suddenly came flying into my bedroom looking for trouble.

"What is wrong with you?" I asked, barely looking up from my new copy of *World Tennis* magazine.

"You want to know what's wrong with me?" she snapped. "I don't like your *attitude.*"

Here we go again, I thought.

"I don't know what you're talking about, just get out of here," I instructed her in my most dismissive tone.

And then she lost it.

"Why don't I ever catch you doing anything good around here?" she screamed, as she methodically ripped each of the "Catch 'Em Doing Good" cards I'd received from my favorite teacher off my wall—one by one like Richard Dreyfuss with Marsha Mason's "panties ... on ... the rod ..." in *The Goodbye Girl*—crumbling them into balls and throwing them on the ground. "Why does *she* always get the good kid and I get stuck with *this?*"

She then stormed out of the room and slammed her bedroom door.

Stunned, I slowly bent down to reach for the floor to pick up ... my jaw ... and the cards—while I was already down there—one by one, using my hands to try to smooth them over. And then later, I tried to smooth things over with my mom, not really sure what had caused her to get so angry and writing it off as her being in one of her "moods."

Nearly a decade later, my best pal from Detroit, Mark, moved to Southern California. Naturally, one of the first things I wanted to do when I visited him was to drive through Benedict Canyon to find "the" house on Cielo Drive, where Tate & Co. met their grisly demise. We arrived late at night, as one tends to do when pursuing one of these macabre ideas, but as we got near the place we sort of panicked and sped off. The last time Mark had been up there, a woman had come out and yelled at him and his friend Robert, who isn't the type to get cold feet about these kinds of things. He drives a hearse. "If you're looking for the Manson house," she screamed, "*this* isn't it!" Being the good nancies that we were, though, we drew the conclusion that it indeed was. Like the slaughter townhouse on South Bundy Drive in Brentwood, where Nicole Brown Simpson and Ron Goldman were butchered on the walkway, the street number has since been changed—and in this case, the house demolished and replaced with a new one, effectively ending my dream of seeing the scene of the crime.

In 1991 (when I, myself, was living on South Bundy Drive), I went home to Phoenix for a visit and ended up accompanying my college friend Debra to a youth event she was producing for Planned Parenthood. Debra had a wonderful young troupe of performers who would act out scenes on topics related to teen issues and the like. As we were leaving the venue packed with teenagers, I heard a familiar voice in the distance screaming out, "Kenny! Kenny! Is that you?" There was Mrs. Carney—or was she Carol by now?—looking exactly as she did when I'd last seen her a dozen years ago: same sassy blonde hairdo, same kind smile. We spoke only briefly—my ride was pulling out, and Mrs. Carney had a hundred kids to round up—but a really warm feeling came over me as we embraced after all those years. Although I still didn't have the nerve to mention *Helter Skelter*—she was *still* Mrs. Carney, after all!—I thanked her for the attention and support she'd given me as a child. When I started school in Arizona after spending the first twelve years of my life in Detroit, I'd felt pretty disconnected. Mrs. Carney made me feel important when I really needed it, filling a need in me that even the best mother in the world could not. It was only at that moment that I realized why my mom went berserk that afternoon in my bedroom, finally seeing through

61

my adult eyes that she was jealous of my relationship with another woman, and hurting that she was missing out on things by going back to work. But sometimes you need to be treated as if you're special by a less partial observer.

(I forgave Mom about the note cards decades ago. Now, if only I could forgive her for another psychotic episode during which she crumbled up a hard-to-come-by photo of Yugoslavian tennis star Mima Jausovec, which was part of my women's tennis rankings that I had displayed on my dresser before I got a bulletin board. What did the 1977 French Open champion ever do to *you,* Mom?)

At the end of that fateful school year, Mrs. Carney awarded me with a certificate for "Best Attitude," an honor I still have in my possession today. The last thing she said to me the day I left Rhodes to go to Dobson High was: "I expect to see your name in lights someday, Kenny." I may not have lived up to her great expectations yet, but her vote of confidence has stayed with me over the years. And I've done everything in my power not to disappoint her, even if the nature of my "attitude" has remained in question ever since.

new balls, please

Growing up, tennis was pretty much my life. After a brief youthful attempt at boxing—a sport that was in the Walsh blood, but should be avoided in Detroit boxing gyms by boys whose best defense is a sharp tongue—my brothers and I came to our senses and hung up our less-than-golden gloves and focused exclusively on tennis. Playing. Taking lessons. Going to tournaments. Reading books and magazines about it. Watching the pros on television. Coming up with my own ranking systems.

We started playing in 1977 when my mom's flirtation with "getting some exercise" petered out after two lessons—why run around getting sweaty when you can smoke cigarettes and be rail thin and gorgeous after having five kids?—and her equipment was left in the basement to gather dust.

Oldest brother Bill started things off, using Mom's racket to hit tennis balls against the wall of a church near our house. (This was the closest my brothers and I have ever come to organized religion.) That summer, Tracy Austin's Cinderella run at Forest Hills got me hooked, and before I knew it I was taking lessons with the big guys over at Rosie's Park in Madison Heights. That our instructor, Fred Kaviuk, looked incredible in super-short white polyester tennis shorts only made me (practice) harder. Between my brothers, my stepfather, and my brother's friends (Paul, Barry, and Mike), there was always a gang going to play tennis.

About a year later, our mom agreed to let Billy, Terence, and me join Village Racquet Club, an indoor facility just across the county line on Chicago Road in Warren, where I spent the next two years battling it out against the other kids on the Junior Improvement Ladder, always looking to make my move onto the Junior Achievement side. That period is one of my favorite times of my childhood. Mom would pick me up in her beige Pontiac Catalina station wagon at Page Middle School, and "Time Passages" by Al Stewart and "Reminiscing" by the Little River Band would *always* come on the radio as we drove directly—right past our house on 13 Mile Road—to the club, where my brothers and I would participate in clinics, use our unlimited "walk-on" court time, and soak in the hot tub in between doing homework in the lounge area. I had a bunch of friends there, and we'd usually stay until closing time, which was far past any normal eleven-year-old's bedtime. I had the life.

By the time we moved to Arizona in the spring of '79—lured to a place we'd never been with the promise of a tennis court in our own backyard—my brothers and I had all been playing competitively for a number of years and were ready for the next big thing. The tennis court turned out not to be *exactly* in our backyard—there were dozens of them throughout the master planned community we lived in—and my brothers and I contemplated a call to Child Protective Services over this bait-and-switch move. (The complaint was never placed.) It also turned out that Phoenix's "perfect" weather actually meant it was 175 degrees each and every day, but by then there was no turning back.

That fall, my brothers and I signed up to play on the Dobson Ranch team tennis league, modeled after the famed World Team Tennis of the '70s. Our team consisted of the Walsh brothers—ages twelve, fourteen, and seventeen—and a man who joined by himself thinking he'd be placed on a team with other adults (singles, perhaps) he could become friends with. (I think poor guy's name was Vaughn Gunter-Smith, and I know he had a *huge* serve.) Instead, he had to deal with a snot-nose kid (me) for three months. Each week, we'd take on another team of feisty housewives with really annoying strokes who somehow managed to be more competitive than Jimmy Connors and Martina Navratilova combined. I'd get frustrated thinking I should be able to kill those hacks (which I usually could do in singles) but then fall apart in doubles where those types seem to excel. I was known to call foot faults on *my own* doubles partner if I wasn't happy with the way things were going, which was invariably the *partner's* fault as far as I was concerned. I was awful, and the whole thing was an unmitigated disaster. I managed to bring home a grand total of three tennis trophies during a lengthy junior career: One was a Mesa Parks and Recreation combined consolation round for ten- and twelve-year-olds, which I won despite lying on the court crying hysterically after blowing a chance to close it out in straight sets. The second was a doubles trophy for the consolation round of the Mesa "Turkey" tournament when I was fifteen. My greatest victory was winning the main draw of our neighborhood association's annual junior event when I was sixteen. I came back from quadruple match point down to win in three exhilarating sets—against a thirteen-year-old *girl.*

In between various tournaments, I played on the junior varsity team at Rhodes Junior High, an experience that came rushing back recently when a childhood friend of mine e-mailed me a team photo he'd come across in an old copy of our school paper he'd packed away. It was a surprisingly unsettling moment.

Part of me was thrilled, of course, having not seen the image in thirty years. To be honest, I'd all but forgotten it even existed—and I'm the guy who saves everything. But as much as I'd like to say that seeing that photo of me and my fellow Rhodes Roadrunners brought back a rush of good memories (I played No. 1 singles and doubles, and we made it to the City Championships in 1981-82), it reminded me of a dark time, when I was subjected to a barrage of homophobic bullying at the hands of my so-called friends, teammates, and coach.

My best friend on the team at the time was Jim Bell. But I had also been close to my teammate Mike Murphy during seventh grade and become even closer to Myk (a "New Wave" spelling he adopted in the mid-'80s, that was simply pronounced "Mike") Mishoe in eighth and ninth grades. (We shared a mutual obsession with microwave bacon, Ringo Starr's *Caveman,* Rick Springfield's "Jessie's Girl," and slasher flicks.) I also had one good friend who wasn't on the team. Greg was a grade behind us, so he wasn't eligible to play yet. But having met through the junior tennis circuit, we played a lot of tennis on the weekends. And because I was one of his only friends, he would occasionally come to my practices to hang out and watch. (Tales of my sidespin forehand sort of had to be seen to be believed.)

Somewhere along the line, Jim and I had become inseparable. Jim was a Southern California native, blond, short, and athletic to my lanky Midwestern persona. While I was always wearing tennis whites, he was super casual, decked out in a pair of Ocean Pacific shorts and Vans, the quintessential surfer boy.

In addition to being best buds on the team, Jim and I began to spend every waking minute together after school, playing tennis, swimming in my backyard, or just hanging out in my room, where he would sleep over nearly every weekend. His single mother was an eccentric Jesus freak who would hand out day-old snack cakes from the Hostess Thrift Store—purchased undoubtedly on what the sign trumpeted as WEDNESDAY *BARGIN* DAY—to homeless people in an attempt to recruit them (Evangelical Sno-Balls?), and I could tell Jim enjoyed being away from that environment as much as possible. That my wacky brood brought normalcy to his life was all I needed to know. I believe his dad lived in Orange County, but fathers were a subject neither of us felt comfortable discussing, which in turn made me feel all the more comfortable with him.

It was a difficult time. It was freshman year of high school, albeit spent in junior high. I'm the only person I know who had the misfortune of spending four long years in junior high, arguably the worst time in anyone's life. It was the byproduct of moving from a Michigan school district where sixth grade was in middle school to an Arizona school district where ninth grade was in middle school. All of my peers were going through the typical things that "normal" puberty-fueled teenagers were going through: first kisses, first dates, first dances, first girlfriends. I, on the other hand, was locked in my bedroom, fixated on the hunky men in my mom's Avon catalogs and sneaking a peek at the hidden-away *Playgirl* she had gotten as a "gag" gift for her fortieth birthday.

What the post-*Will & Grace* generation doesn't understand is that for many years, it wasn't even a matter of being "in" or "out" of the closet: I honestly didn't even know what "being gay" *was*. All I knew was that I couldn't stop dreaming about Christopher Atkins in *The Blue Lagoon,* and that I kept a photo of a Miles O'Keefe from the Bo Derek remake of *Tarzan* under my mattress. (Shockingly, I am loincloth-fetish-free today.) And that clearly made me very different. Certain there was no one else who felt the way I did, I figured I would eventually marry a woman and just pretend I didn't feel the way I did. It was an incredibly alienating time, yet somehow Jim made me feel as if I was normal.

When I finally got my first hint about what this "difference" was, it was not reassuring. Billie Jean King, who eight years earlier had dazzled a worldwide television audience of 90 million by crushing Bobby Riggs in the infamous 1973 "Battle of the Sexes," was now being sued for palimony by a former lover—her *female* hairdresser. The media went into overdrive, and so did my brain. Billie Jean King was married: What could this possibly mean? After initially denying the allegations, King held a televised press conference to address them. My parents had it on, but I was too mortified to watch it with them, just as I had been when Billy Crystal came on the screen during episodes of *Soap.* So I snuck upstairs to the loft above our living room to watch from a safe distance while my parents—and the rest of the world—gawked below. I don't think they knew I was up there listening. It wasn't until the exact moment that Billie Jean uttered the word "homosexual" that I had a name for what it was that made me different. Homosexual? Wow! That's what I am.

Although it seems funny now that it would be news Billie Jean King was a lesbian, in 1981 things were very different. It was a scandal. Sponsors were threatening to drop the women's tennis tour. Billie Jean lost all of her personal endorsements. Famous people just didn't admit to being gay—even if they were. So as she fessed up to the affair—hubby Larry and her mortified parents looking on—she made a point of stressing that as a married woman, she felt she had erred by having an affair regardless of its being heterosexual or homosexual in nature. Years later she said her PR team begged her not to hold the press conference, but that she was raised by her "deeply homophobic" parents to always tell the truth. The irony was not lost on her.

Despite her outing, Billie Jean stayed married for some time after that, even telling the press at one point that she and Larry were considering adopting a baby. But they eventually divorced, and after dodging the subject in print for seventeen years, she *finally* officially came out in *The Advocate* in its August 18, 1998, issue.

But for me, the press conference was a watershed moment. Although nothing really changed in my day-to-day life, I finally knew what I was working with. Although I felt no sexual attraction toward Jim—he was like a brother to me—it was a relief having a friend who was "like me" just by virtue of the fact that he wasn't girl crazy and he liked the same things I did. There was a strong bond forming between us; we'd even started playing doubles tournaments together away from school. (He was my partner at the November "Turkey tourney.") Things were looking up as my first year of high school loomed.

Then one day, seemingly out of nowhere, Jim turned on me. He'd grown cold in the previous weeks, but never in my most dramatic teenage nightmare had I imagined he was busy spearheading an ultimatum that would alter the course of my existence.

Like a scene out of a John Hughes flick, Jim showed up at my house one day after school and knocked on the door. My friend Greg was there, so Greg slipped into the den off the entryway to give us some privacy.

I opened the door and without even saying hello—much less coming inside—Jim asked me point-blank to choose between Greg and the tennis team. According to Jim, the team had been discussing the matter, and they didn't like it when Greg came to our practices. He was a "fag" and they didn't want him hanging out with us. (Apparently Molly wasn't the only one who had figured Greg out.)

I couldn't understand what was really going on here. Was this their way of telling me they thought I was gay? (After all, I did model my game after Chris Evert Lloyd's.) And even if it wasn't, they were making it clear that being gay—as they had most certainly decided Greg was—was not acceptable. Just as Billie Jean King had been dropped by her sponsors after her admission, I too was beginning to see that being gay came at a price.

But still, without hesitation, I chose Greg, who had been nothing but a great friend to me from the day we'd met, not to mention the single funniest person I have ever met. I may have been shocked and terrified by what was happening—it seemed the walls were closing in on my fourteen-year-old world—but I had been raised to know the difference between right and wrong.

Jim left quietly. But then overnight, I went from being a reasonably popular part of the gang to having my phone ring at all hours of the night with each team member calling me up asking me in their best "Greg voices"—which even my mom had noted for its "fruitiness"—if they could come over tonight "to have sex," then bursting into hysterical laughter. I was horrified ... and terrified. How long before they said something directly to my family? On top of everything, our coach not only did nothing to discourage this behavior; he participated in it, going so far as to get on the phone to taunt me.

From there, I was completely ostracized by the team, and I spent the remainder of the season sitting alone on the bus en route to away meets, skipping post-practice outings to Peter Piper Pizza, and attending an awards ceremony in which no one on the team uttered a word to me. I would have invited my parents to attend—our team had done really well—but it would have been mortifying for them to see that the only award I was going to bring home that night was "Most Likely to Be a Fag." It was one of those rare moments I was glad my mom had no use for school events.

Making matters exponentially worse during this entire traumatic period was the fact that I was also dealing with the discovery of a huge mass on my left testicle. I had noticed it a year or two beforehand, and had tried everything I could to convince myself that nothing was wrong. But then my worst fears were confirmed, sort of. During a mandatory tennis team physical at school—all us boys lined up and dropping trou in the coaches' locker room office area—the man (a doctor or an eager "volunteer"?) with the rubber glove squeezed my abnormal ball and told me I needed to see a urologist "immediately." To me, he looked disgusted.

I was different, so of course my privates were too, my adolescent brain reasoned. He could tell I was gay just by looking at me down there. In my shame and fear, I told no one. I diagnosed myself with testicular cancer—something pro tennis player Butch Waltz had been battling around this time—and convinced myself it was caused by my disgusting secret, that I was sexually attracted to other boys, the same secret that had now cost me my friends. The physical was prior to the start of season, so I'd spent the entire year expecting our coach to pull me aside to follow up on the doctor's orders. But that conversation never occurred, so I never went to the doctor.

The tennis season was over, and I did not go back. For the remaining years of high school, I fended off questions from friends and family about why I wasn't on the tennis team anymore—tennis was my life, after all—but I could only make up vague excuses about being "too busy." Not long after, someone pointed out a large bump on my forehead. I had never really noticed it before, but when it was brought to my attention, I became convinced my cancer had spread, and I now had a brain tumor. I was in a perpetual state of panic, denial, and bangs. I spent the next seven years thinking each night that I would likely die in my sleep from this slow-growing but now spreading "tumor," yet did nothing to stop it. The rejection I'd experienced for (probably) being gay convinced me I would be better off dead.

While the whole thing seems difficult to believe now—even for me—you'd be surprised what fear and self-loathing can do to a young boy's mind. The experience was a living nightmare that colors the way I view the world to this day. It wasn't until I was twenty years old that I finally got up the nerve to see a doctor. I hadn't died yet. And I'd finally met some other gay guys in college and realized I wanted to stick around, so I figured it was time. But even doing that was incredibly traumatic.

I tried more than a dozen times to speak to my mom directly about the problem, but I just could not bring myself to say it. She had already been through so much—abandoned by both parents, an abusive husband, losing a baby—and the thought of telling her that her son was possibly dying from being a homo was just too much for me to bear.

Instead, I left a handwritten note on the refrigerator door one morning. My poor parents discovered it over breakfast en route to work, then came racing into my room. They sweetly comforted me, then cleared their schedules to immediately take me to the local family medical practice. There, a doctor informed me that I had a varicocele, an unsightly but completely benign condition caused by an enlargement of the vein that drains the testicle. The only possible complication from my "life-threatening" condition was that it could reduce my sperm count—the veins make your nuts warmer, which is bad for sperm production—and that was all I needed to hear. This had *nothing* to do with being gay. There was an operation to cure my condition, but unless conceiving children became an issue, it was considered entirely cosmetic. Oh, and the "tumor" on my forehead? Turns out the cancer hadn't metastasized. My skull had just been permanently reshaped by a wooden cotton candy display that fell off the ceiling above the movie-theater concession stand I was working at in high school. They gave me a free Nestle Crunch bar when I came to—covered in Coke syrup and popcorn kernels—as a settlement for my workplace injury. And lest you think I should have gotten a lawyer, those candy bars at AMC theaters cost *a lot.*

My parents still didn't know about my sexuality, but the albatross that had been living in my tighty whities was now gone. I walked out of the doctor's office that morning feeling for the first time as if I truly had my whole life ahead of me.

Many years later, I learned through the grapevine that the homo-hating ringleader Jim was—you guessed it—gay, and it was only then that the whole thing began to make sense.

With Dan Savage and hubby Terry Miller's "It Gets Better" campaign in full swing a few years ago, I had to ask myself: Did it get better? It did. But I had the resources to further my education and to move to a place where my sexuality is less of an issue. Not everyone is so fortunate. And many of the stories I hear about today do not sound that much different from what I went through thirty years ago—when my sexuality left me feeling abandoned and allowed me to ignore serious concerns about my health in what a friend later called a "passive suicide attempt." Gay kids are still being bullied for who they are and are killing themselves at a rate that is shockingly higher than average. And that breaks my heart all over again.

A couple of summers ago, after years of residual fear, embarrassment, and procrastination, I finally decided to have my varicocele removed. My urologist informed me that mine was the biggest he'd ever seen—gee, thanks; the first time anyone's ever said that when my drawers were dropped—but that the surgery was completely routine.

"Save for a small incision in your pubic region," he said, "it'll be like it was never there."

Decades in the making, and what happened? The surgery failed.

"This has never happened to me before," my surgeon insisted, a line I thought was reserved for '70s sex comedies.

It somehow seemed fitting, so I just had to laugh. The surgery is a complicated procedure, and one missed vein will make the whole thing fail.

I went in for a correction the following January, and the surgery was a complete success, closing one of the darkest chapters of my life. The only thing that would have made it better would be Jim Bell waiting for me in the recovery room. I finally have the balls to tell him what I really think of him.

hi, anxiety

There's no good reason I should remember January 29, 1982, as well as I do. It wasn't the date of a special birthday or anniversary or anything fun like that. I was in the ninth grade when I happened to see Kate Jackson—Charlie's "smart" angel—on *The Tonight Show With Johnny Carson.*

She was adorable and chatted with Johnny for a bit before he asked her to explain the plot of her new movie, *Making Love,* which she was there to promote.

The audience had no idea this film was Hollywood's first attempt at a big-budget mainstream gay film, but I definitely did. Ever since I'd seen Harry Hamlin and Michael Ontkean in the commercial and poster, it was pretty much all I could think about. Billie Jean King's palimony suit may have been detrimental in many ways, but it had one positive unintended consequence: I knew what "being gay" meant, and I was finally seeing that I wasn't alone. (This is the power of the media that GLAAD talks about.)

The trailer—which I believe I saw before Woody Allen's *A Midsummer Night's Sex Comedy*—hadn't even shown any of the film's stars before it delivered a written warning of sorts. The following appeared on-screen, and this gay boy was raring to go:

Twentieth Century Fox is proud to present one of the most honest and controversial films we have ever released. We believe MAKING LOVE breaks new ground in its sensitive portrayal of a young woman executive who learns her husband is experiencing a crisis about his sexual identity. MAKING LOVE deals openly and candidly with a delicate issue. It is not sexually explicit. But it may be too strong for some people. MAKING LOVE is bold but gentle. We are proud of its honesty. We applaud its courage. MAKING LOVE: a love story for the '80s.

Knowing that she was entering uncharted territory, Kate—like the trailer itself—tried to ease the crowd into things. She told the audience that the film was about "something new that you might not have a lot experience with" but that it was "a love story about a married man who has an affair ... with another *man.*"

And that was all they needed to hear. It didn't take more than a second for the audience to turn on her—and turn *hard.* They began to boo her—one of Charlie's Angels! The *smart* one!—on national television. They were enraged. I was stunned, flabbergasted. Was this actually happening? I had to ask myself. Was this actually going down right here in my living room? It was as if there had just been a referendum on me on network television, and the vote was a resounding no.

Johnny had to step in, reprimand the audience, and force them to be nice. He calmed the people in the audience down. Kate maintained her composure and proceeded to show the clip of the scene where she throws the white kitchen plate because she can't stand her husband's silence anymore. The audience politely clapped when it was over, but by then the collective emotional damage had been done. Here I was, a confused fourteen-year-old boy who had only recently discovered there was a term for the unconventional sexual feelings he had been anxiously hiding all these years, and then the second someone so much as broached the topic, it was met with contempt and disgust.

If police raids on gay bars in the '50s and '60s and Anita Bryant and the Briggs Initiative (aka Prop 6) in the '70s had pushed gay people back into the closet before me, I can't help but wonder how many people that one guest spot on *The Tonight Show* pushed back into the closet in the '80s.

I say there's no good reason for me to remember January 29, 1982, but that's not entirely true. Through years of self-analysis—and a little professional—I now realize that was a date with huge historical significance in my life. It's the day my entire sense of self changed. If Billie Jean had (however inadvertently) quietly emboldened me even one bit by helping me realize I was not alone in my feelings, that episode of *The Tonight Show* confirmed every feeling of self-loathing the tennis-team ordeal had instilled in me. My ability not to be painfully self-conscious around people ended that night, and social anxiety disorder took over my life. I can readily call it social anxiety disorder today—or SAD, as it should be referred to for short but isn't thanks to those bullshit Seasonal Affective Disorder people—but that diagnosis wouldn't come for another two decades, leaving me to fend for myself.

What had started as somewhat typical "embarrassing" teenage moments—when parents' friends would ask if you "like girls yet" or "have a girlfriend"—turned into crippling anxiety after seeing that hostile reaction to homosexuality on *Johnny Carson*. Instead of brushing off such inquiries, which plague plenty of socially awkward straight kids as well, I began to avoid all situations that could lead down this path. My self-doubt and increasing sense of worthlessness—the whole nation would turn hostile and boo me if they knew who I really was—became who I was. All a stranger had to say to me was "Hi," and I'd instantly turn beet red and my heart would start racing out of control. Suddenly, I would have the makings of a full-fledged panic attack. It was a complete 180 for the kid who used to be able to walk up to any stranger's house and sell them anything, and I was suffering deeply.

No one had any clue about what I was going through. I was still the cute, smart kid with the Toni Tennille 'do to the outside world. But navigating ways to minimize my exposure became an every-waking-hour crisis. My biggest issue was the blushing, which became even more problematic when I started wearing glasses. I would become so flushed that my lenses would steam up to the point that I could literally not see through them. This would understandably confuse coworkers who had merely asked me how my weekend had been. The anticipation of this happening fueled even more panic, and I began to choreograph getting up to fetch something or rearranging something on a table or shelf as I gave answers, in the hope that there would be less focus on my burning-red face.

While everyone close to me will likely swear that none of this is true—isolation being the heinous hallmark of most anxiety disorders, and I never seemed to be isolated—there also isn't one person in my life who can't vividly recall an inexplicable moment when I seemed to react inappropriately to something mundane. The ones who acknowledged anything (my blushing was legendary) would invariably say how "cute it was" when I blushed. (My sister, Jennifer, still talks about how "hilarious" it was the time my family toured Northern Arizona University in 1984, and I turned bright red when I had to tell the tour guide what I planned to "major in" in front of a group of kids and parents.) Yet I was secretly exploring medical solutions, first taking beta blockers and then considering endoscopic transthoracic sympathectomy, a surgical process by which the sympathetic nerves are burned, clamped, and removed in an effort to stem blushing.

Over the years, promotions were avoided. Relationships were compromised. And a general anxiety loomed over everything I did. One afternoon I was riding in the passenger seat while an old boyfriend was driving. We were lost, so he pulled up alongside someone who happened to be on my side, so we could ask for directions. My guy rolled down my window—I was closer to the person, so it made sense for me to do the talking—but I literally could not bring myself to speak. My boyfriend was confused and frustrated, then became angry when I offered no explanation for my bizarre behavior, thinking that I was making him "do" everything. I was in a full-blown meltdown, but I never told him. I did keep seeking help, though.

While most doctors were pretty glib about my trauma—"You know, you've been here twenty-five minutes, and I haven't seen you blush once," they'd say, not realizing that the only time I wouldn't have attacks was when I was comfortable enough with someone to tell them about my problem—by the late '90s medicine seemed to be taking the issue more seriously. It didn't come a moment too soon.

In the summer of 2001, a friend invited me to be his guest at a huge "gay fabulous" pool party in the Hamptons. The event was notorious—the property was enormous, with sex in the bushes, sex in the pool, and a faux bathhouse set up in the basement—so I was thrilled to be going. We arrived at the glamorous home of my friend's friend—he lived on the property adjacent to the pool-party hosts—and unpacked for our weekend of debauchery.

Up until this time, I had learned to negotiate gay social outings pretty well. While I won't say alcohol was particularly helpful for me—if it had been, I'd be a full-fledged alcoholic by now, but I'm a lightweight—it did put me at ease when *everyone else* was a little "happy." It helped that bars and nightclubs were typically dark, so they'd become pretty comfortable places for me. (If a tree blushes in a forest but it's too dark for anyone to notice it ...)

I knew my friend's friend and was fairly comfortable around him, but what I hadn't anticipated was a house full of *other* guests, one more handsome and fabulous than the next. (This was the Hamptons, after all. The next time I stayed at this home, Gayle King was my housemate for the weekend, crashing there to attend Russell Simmons's annual gala.) After coming downstairs for breakfast and meeting all the other guys—everyone completely friendly, everyone making typical small talk—a surge of panic overtook me as it never had before.

Someone would ask where I lived, and my heart would race. Someone would ask me what I did for a living, and I would turn red and sweat profusely. By the time someone asked me where I was from, I could no longer breathe. I quickly excused myself and returned to my in-suite bathroom, where I splashed water on my burning face and attempted to regroup, then attempted unsuccessfully to return to eat. I later willed myself to attend the pool party—it helped that another housemate from Australia volunteered that he was feeling horribly anxious—but I spent every other moment tucked away in my room pretending to be tired and not feeling well.

What had started as a youthful fear of people finding out I was gay—surely if I opened my mouth, anyone would immediately "know about" me, as we called it then—had taken over every aspect of my life. When I came out in my early twenties, I had hoped this would "set me free," only to find out the damage had been done. Like Pavlov's dog, there was no going back. It was as if the irrational fear of rejection had been embedded in my DNA.

Although I'd majored in journalism in college, I'd given up any hopes of being a reporter since approaching strangers for a living was an unthinkable prospect. (Copy editing seemed like the safest substitute.)

That fall, I revisited my doctor, who could see by the look in my eyes that I was truly traumatized by what had happened that weekend in the Hamptons. If my doctor had been dismissive before, this time he could not have been more serious.

I was prescribed a selective serotonin reuptake inhibitor (or SSRI)—a class of antidepressants frequently used to treat depression, anxiety disorders, and even some personality disorders. (Some found my personality to be disorderly, I figured, so why not kill two birds with one stone?) My life improved quickly and exponentially.

Today, I'm no longer consumed with anxiety and fear of social settings. I began pursuing career goals that I thought I would never be able to tackle. I even did some newspaper reporting—twenty years after I should have gotten my start. (It turns out I dislike it for completely different reasons!)

I wouldn't say I'm "cured." I still "go red" more easily than the average person. But it's nothing like it was before. In fact, the changes have been so natural that I started to believe I wasn't benefiting from the drugs anymore (a not-atypical belief by people with psychological disorders, I've been told) and went off them a few years ago. Almost overnight, I began to have panic attacks around colleagues with whom I'd been working for years. It was as shocking as it was eye-opening. Whatever is wrong with me is wired deep inside me now, short-circuited that night Kate Jackson appeared on *The Tonight Show.*

It took about twenty-five years for this horrifying memory to begin to fade a bit; then Heath Ledger and Jake Gyllenhaal made the talk-show rounds in 2005 to promote *Brokeback Mountain,* which was arguably the long-awaited follow-up to *Making Love.*

With its huge box-office gross and countless awards, *Brokeback* was America's chance to treat the subject of homosexuality with respect and to show how much this country had progressed since 1982. America finally got the opportunity to not ridicule the film's participants—Oprah treated the cast as if they were promoting any major movie—and to make amends to the Kate Jacksons of the '80s and the outcasts who sat at home and watched in horror. And while no gay films have come anywhere close to matching the success of *Brokeback Mountain,* it's no coincidence that everything about the cultural landscape has changed for the LGBT community since its success. This alone makes me a lot less anxious.

For thirty years, part of me has always wondered if I might have imagined the whole *Tonight Show* debacle. I've looked for it on YouTube and even visited the Museum of Radio and Television History to see if I could get a glimpse, but to no avail. Then recently a reader of my blog e-mailed me a link to the clip, which immediately sent my heart racing.

It took me a good half hour to get up the nerve to watch it, but when I did, I was amazed by how the human brain "remembers" things.

For starters, David Brenner was the guest host that night, yet I vividly recall Johnny Carson coming to Kate's aid. (I also used to think David Brenner was funny, but ... wow.) And then there was the incident. Being older and having a thicker skin now, I would have to admit that it wasn't nearly as bad as I recall. The booing in my memory went on for what felt like hours, so I suppose there's no way it could have been that bad. In fact, it was Kate who kind of hesitated when she told the audience what the film was about, almost inviting them to give a thumbs-up or thumbs-down to the topic of homosexuality. A small but vocal minority did boo, but Brenner quickly dismissed them with a rather odd comeback: "There's a guy from Utah who sucks wood." What stands out more now is that Jackson was there to promote her new major motion picture, yet Brenner seemed extremely hesitant to bring it up. It wasn't until about eight minutes into the interview—when the clock had all but run out—that he belatedly "remembered" to ask her about the film. The clip I recalled from the film was indeed shown, but then the interview was over. This was clearly not an accident.

Despite the fact that it wasn't "as bad" as I remembered, it still made me sick all over again, thinking about that isolated fourteen-year-old boy watching television that night and getting booed over his shameful secret. If it seems like almost nothing now, that's just further proof that it's the little things that can affect people so much, especially children. Things are hardly perfect for gay youths today. Still, I'm glad something this blatant would be unlikely to happen again.

hot nights, hot nights

They say you never forget your first love, and I'm certainly no exception—even if the reasons aren't quite what Aphrodite had in mind.

Derek was the perfect first boyfriend: tall, broad-shouldered, and handsome, plus slightly older and far more experienced—exactly what this sexually repressed boy from suburbia needed. We met at a graduation party for a mutual friend, and the chemistry between us was instantaneous. He playfully approached me and my friends and asked if we were going to be "cliquish" all night, or "play nice" with the others. I admired his boldness. And with his brown eyes and dark hair boyishly falling on his forehead, he looked like a cross between John Cusack and Ferris Bueller, with a sporty hint of D.B. Sweeney thrown in for good measure. I was smitten. Moments later we were making out in the bathroom down the hall, before going fishing in each other's pants in a boat parked on the side of the house. We tripped the house alarm, but unfortunately I was too swept away for other alarms to go off, most notably that Derek's ex-boyfriend was lurking in the shadows, an ex with whom he had broken up moments earlier.

The next month was a whirlwind of firsts: mostly carnal, some chemical, and many emotional. Again, the economy-sized bottle of lubricant that didn't have enough left in it for my virginity-breaking romp managed to raise no red flags. I was madly in love with the guy. I had had a grand total of one fling in my twenty years of life, but Steve was more incidental than monumental, a guy who hit on me one night when I used my brother Terence's ID to go to a gay bar downtown. How could I *not* go home with Steve that night at the Connection? He'd dedicated Taylor Dayne's "Tell It to My Heart" to me.

Derek, by contrast, was the real thing. He was all I could think about and all I wanted to think about.

Not even a month into our meeting was my twenty-first birthday. I already had my present, but Derek planned a surprise party, even arranging for my childhood friends from Detroit—Mark, Brad, and J.R.—to fly in for the occasion, plus everyone else I knew. The party was the happiest night of my life up until that point—straight out of a John Hughes movie that had never had a role for me—complete with kegs, and friends surreptitiously hooking up in bedrooms and smoking pot in the tool shed on the side of the house: all the things I'd heard about in high school but was never a part of. My parents just happened to be out of town that weekend, which was the cherry on the teen-movie cake. That I later found out Derek had originally planned to have the soiree in a suite at the resort where he worked but had to quietly move it to my parents' house after getting kicked out of the place for having a blowout pre-party only added to his alluring bad-boy image.

When my mom and Gary returned from their trip and found all of my childhood friends crashing at our house, they kindly took everybody out to my favorite Thai restaurant to celebrate my "being legal." On the way to the Pink Pepper, my mom was eager to hear the details of my friends' coming to surprise me, so she turned to look over her shoulder to talk to Mark, J.R., and me in the back seat of her Oldsmobile Calais. My stepfather was blasting the *Dirty Dancing* soundtrack, so my mom lowered the volume so we could talk.

"Hey, I like this song!" Gary protested, turning the volume back up even louder to make his point, as my mom struggled to hear us over Patrick Swayze's dramatic weather-related simile. As if she'd practiced a thousand times, Mom simultaneously hit the eject button on the tape deck and the down button on the power window, then tossed the *Dirty*

Dancing cassette out onto South Dobson Road. This time, Mark's only tears would be from laughter.

But no sooner did Derek and I exchange "I love yous" than he announced he was quitting his job at a resort in Scottsdale and moving up to Seattle for the summer with his friend Kelly. Kelly had recently fallen in love too, and was bringing Alan with him. Derek was going solo—I couldn't quit my job on a lark, anyway—and he was already begging me to come up for a visit.

After a month of daily phone calls and a barrage of letters and postcards, I was finally en route to the Pacific Northwest. Derek was originally from Oregon, but this was my first time in the region, and Seattle had become the hot spot of the late '80s.

The trip was intoxicating—if falling in love for the first time was exciting, being reunited in a majestic new city with your first love was even more so—and when he moved back to Phoenix at the end of the summer and asked me to move in with him, the alienation of my gay youth seemed to vanish.

I was starting my senior year of college, and Derek had been hired to be the room-service manager at the newly opening Ritz-Carlton in the Biltmore section of Phoenix, one of the city's toniest addresses. Derek had found an apartment in Central Phoenix (on 38th Street and Thomas, just a few buildings away from our good friend Kurt), and I was thrilled to be going to school by day and playing house by night with my suit-and-tied boyfriend.

My brother Terence had recently moved and could no longer have a cat, so Derek and I adopted Lou, and a family unit started to form, something I had only recently come to realize was possible for two men after seeing the film *Parting Glances,* where lovers Michael and Robert dealt with the same ups and downs as every other couple I had seen. Derek later surprised me with a kitten, a tabby we named Phillip, then Derek surprised the landlord with an un-house-trained yellow lab puppy we called Dakota. I was twenty-one, had landed a coveted internship at the state's top paper, the *Arizona Republic,* and was living with the man of my dreams. What could possibly go wrong?

Then one afternoon, I decided to surprise Derek by getting the two rolls of film he had sitting in an odds 'n' ends basket on top of the refrigerator developed. I took them to a one-hour-photo-developing business near our apartment—it was "Free Double Prints Tuesday"—not realizing I was the one who was in for a surprise.

It turned out the pictures were from his "summer spent desperately missing me" in Seattle—and while I wish I could say I was the kind of guy who was able to find comfort in learning he had managed to console himself in my absence with a young sandy-haired guy who looked remarkably like me, I instead drove to the Ritz-Carlton to give Derek a surprise of his own.

I went racing over to the hotel, brakes screeching as I arrived at the entrance, where the valet parkers all laughed not-quite-under-their-breath at my "girl" car—a white Volkswagen Convertible Rabbit, natch—then took my claim check and went flying into the lobby. Derek happened to be right in the vicinity, but sensing something was horribly wrong, he found a place where we could speak in private.

With the most incriminating photo already in my hand, I let loose.

"Who the hell is this?" I demanded, suddenly realizing we were in one of the hotel's most opulent banquet rooms, which perfectly matched my feeling that I was channeling a crushed Michele Lee in a made-for-TV movie.

Stunned, Derek took a moment to answer.

"He's just a friend," he finally responded, his nervous laughter telling me everything I needed to know.

But within a few minutes, he had artfully turned the whole thing around on me—"How dare you come to my place of employment and accuse me of something like this?"—and I was on my way home.

By bedtime, Derek—the consummate charmer and salesperson that he was—had "convinced" me that the guy was indeed just a friend, and that the cozy-looking "arm around him" pose was just something he did "out of habit" when he set the timer of the camera.

I Jackie Kennedy–ed myself into looking the other way, but a few weeks later I discovered an unfamiliar pair of Calvin Klein briefs in our laundry. Hesitant to make another accusation, I phoned my friend Mark in Orange County to seek counsel.

"Who the fuck is this skinny ass?" I asked distraughtly, noticing the size 28 tag in the tighty-whities, too small for even my runway-ready 6-foot, 135-pound frame. Panicked and determined not to destroy my "happy home"—was it any wonder I related so well to middle-aged women in grade school?—I avoided a confrontation, only to have Derek turn around and inform me that we "needed to talk." Thanksgiving break was coming up, and he told me that he was feeling a little bit confused—and wanted a "Thanksgiving break" of his own to mull things over.

"I just need one week to think things over," he told me, trying to act as if this were the most normal thing for couples to do.

"Is there somebody else?" I asked, still reeling from the double dose of double prints and dubious drawers.

"No, no," he reassured me, "of course not."

"Well, what are the ground rules for this 'trial separation'?" I demanded to know. "Are we allowed to see other people?" This moment would later be referred to as Kenneth the Journalist at Work, always demanding to know the five *w*'s and one *h*: who, what, where, when, why, and how.

"That's not what this is about, Kenneth," he said, somewhat incredulously. "I'm not going to see anyone else. I just need some time to clear my head."

And with that, I agreed to his request.

But I was crushed. Although the idea of two guys in their

very early twenties falling in love and spending their lives together seems pretty preposterous now, my closeted and repressed puberty had missed out on all the typical milestones—first kiss, first date, first love—so I had every fiber of myself invested in this relationship, and that left me extraordinarily vulnerable. Derek had had girlfriends in high school and had fooled around with boys all the way back to his scouting days. But when he finally realized what he truly desired, he held back nothing. Although I think I was special to him in some way, I was also just "the latest" guy in his life.

Distraught, I moved back into my old bedroom at my parents' house, pretending I had come home "for the holidays." This would have been a perfectly plausible cover for a college student if not for the fact that my apartment with Derek was a mere ten-minute drive away. By day two of the "trial separation," I could no longer breathe, so I showed up unannounced at the homestead convinced that the mere sight of me would make him beg me to come home. Instead, I was greeted by a towel-around-the-waist-clad Derek—"Hey, Kenneth. How are you?"—who kept one arm leaning on the door frame to keep me from coming in as he attempted to make small talk.

I still had my keys, but out of *respect* I knocked on the door, and this is the way he treats me? I thought, as I pushed my way in.

I quickly went from room to room taking stock of the situation, not entirely sure what I was looking for. I was a stark-raving lunatic, but a sense of calm came over me when I realized our bottle of lubricant was still sitting in its place in the bathroom. Somehow this convinced me that Derek had been truthful—he wasn't cheating on me or looking for a way out—and I tried to play off the whole visit with a "Just wanted to come by and say Happy Thanksgiving" as I walked out the door. How thoughtful, I was sure he was thinking, as I pulled out of the apartment complex's parking lot.

But as soon as I got home, I felt completely helpless

again. Thanksgiving dinner—a normally festive time at my family's home, as it's one of only three meals my mom routinely cooks each year—had a dark cloud over it. I've always been the most outgoing member of our family, so when I didn't try to lead the conversation or bring any holiday cheer to the table, no one knew what to do. I wanted desperately to stop obsessing, but it was not within my abilities. That no one in my family had any idea what was going on—they didn't even officially know that I was gay, let alone that I was in the midst of a traumatic trial separation—only made me feel isolated and alienated from everyone.

By the time it got dark, I'd decided I couldn't take any more. It had been a good nine or ten hours since I had last barged in on Derek, so another visit was overdue.

I excused myself from the holiday festivities and jumped in my fag-mobile and made record time to our 38th Street digs. The roads were virtually empty, as everyone else was home being thankful for what they had. All I could think about was what I might be losing.

As I got to our apartment complex, I quickly spotted Derek's white Mazda pickup truck in our assigned parking space. I parked and ran up the stairs, deadbolt key already out of my pocket and ready to enter. There would be no "courtesy" knock this time.

My heart was racing as I turned the key, and when I saw the apartment was pitch black, I wondered if Derek had gone out for some turkey and stuffing. But as I took a right down the hall to our bedroom, I realized Derek was indeed enjoying some stuffing of his own—stuffing his penis into the rear end of a tiny person whose face I could not see.

It was a whore show.

"What is going on here?" I demanded, almost confused by what I was seeing.

A startled Derek rolled off of his mysterious "friend," an Asian figure who appeared to be the famous "Napalm girl," only with a bowl cut. But this one was screaming "Too hot!

89

Too hot!" about getting rammed up the ass by my boyfriend, not a helpless child escaping a burning Vietnamese village.

Still confused—was this person even an adult? Where had he come from?—it all began to make sense to me, from the late nights at work, the size 28 underwear in the hamper, and the sudden need for space. This was Fred, a coworker of Derek's from the hotel. In an instant, I became enraged—moving into the living room and ripping the very heavy black retro dial-phone out of the wall and then throwing it just above the headboard, as I screamed, "You fucking son-of-a-bitch liar! I can't wait to call Mike Casola and see what he thinks of *this*!"

Mike Casola, of course, being Derek's boss at the Ritz-Carlton, who I—for reasons that are not entirely clear to me—decided would be the last person Derek and his "friend" would want to know about this liaison. Although gay guys have been working in the hospitality industry since Adam and Eve opened the first Applebee's, being out at work was still not all that commonplace in the '80s, especially in a conservative state like Arizona.

And with that junior-high threat, I made my dramatic exit, barreling down the stairs and down to the parking lot, wishing I could somehow undo what I had just seen. I knew I was in no condition to drive, so I began to run to our friend Kurt's, just up the street. As if the moment was not dramatic enough, it began to violently rain, and as I ran up 38th I noticed Derek was chasing after me, in nothing but boxer shorts, a T-shirt, and bare feet.

I let him catch me—my pathetic self still wanted him to say he loved me and only me—but when he finally got to me, what little spine I was still being held upright with looked him in the eye and said: "Do you know *who* I am? You're going to regret this one day, Derek."

Looking stunned—I'm not even sure what I meant by that—and with a hurt puppy-dog look in his eyes, he replied: "I think I already do."

the best part of breaking up …

With most couples, splitting up doesn't take the first time, and Derek and I were certainly no exception. We spent six months apart after our initial breakup—me as an intern on Capitol Hill working for a congressman from Brooklyn, him working at a resort in Naples, Florida—but he contacted me upon my return from Washington.

When I got back to Phoenix, I had no choice but to move in with my parents since Derek had given up our apartment to follow a friend to the Panhandle State. Things were incredibly tense with my mom. After being initially supportive of my coming out, she began lashing out at me, suddenly insisting that my homosexuality was something I had chosen. I tried to avoid conflict, staying out of her way as much as possible. In addition to taking two summer-school classes to make up for credits I missed while I was in Washington, I also returned to the *Arizona Republic* to work as a correspondent—sort of a continuation of my internship from the previous year—and took a part-time job at a nearby bakery-café in Scottsdale. The manager, a bright and engaging woman named Cat, and I immediately hit it off—Mrs. Carney might have even been the jealous one this time!—and when I told Cat during the interview that I wanted to be a waiter because I thought every writer needed to be one at some point, she was impressed. (Just not impressed enough to let someone with no experience have the job: She made me a cashier.)

Despite classes, homework, and working seven days a week—if I wasn't at the paper, I was at the café—I still found time to carry my torch for Derek, now known as "Derwood" to all of my friends. Derek had grown tired of Naples and the entire Southwest coast of Florida—"nothing but grouchy blue-haired women," he complained—and he abruptly moved to St. Thomas to take a job at the Stouffer Grand Beach Resort. He must have been feeling lonely down there, because he once again launched a full-scale charm offensive, writing me dozens of romantic letters and calling me several times a day, with no regard to the hour.

My exasperated stepfather beat me to the phone on one drunken 2 a.m. call, and asked Derek: "Do you know what time it is?"

"Yes, it's two," Derek replied. "Now, may I speak to Kenneth?"

My summer classes were to finish at the end of July, so Derek asked me to come visit for the month of August, right up until my fall, and final, semester began. Still infatuated beyond reason, I worked and studied night and day, saving up for the big reunion in the romantic U.S. Virgin Islands. Despite having grown up with a swimming pool in our backyard in Phoenix, it was the first—and last—time this pasty Irish-American ever actually attempted to get a base tan. The Arizona sun was brutal, but I would lie out in it for twenty to thirty minutes a day after class, determined to look my best, for my St. Thomas splash. My friends were exhausted by my constant Derek talk, but they really had no choice but to go along. It was all I could think about or talk about, and the truth was, Derek was incredibly sweet and charming to them, too, so they understood why I was so weak around him. Unlike me, though, they knew better.

Just as I was heading to the travel agency to buy my ticket, I phoned Derek to go over my intended itinerary one final time before I made it official. The hotel had put Derek up in one of its rooms while he looked for an apartment, but he hadn't found anything decent yet.

"Hello?" a feminine-sounding voice with a Southern twang answered in his room.

Stunned, I paused before regrouping: "Ah, is Derek there?" My heart was racing, as if I had just walked in on my boyfriend fucking an Asian in our bed.

"No," he replied. "Can I take a message?"

"No message," I said. I hung up and immediately phoned the hotel's front desk and had Derek paged.

From there, Derek launched into a head-spinning, head-scratching story of sex, lies, and Acquired Immune Deficiency Syndrome. The whole thing went something like this:

The guy who'd answered the phone was named David. He and Derek had had a fling while Derek was living in Fort Lauderdale, where he had moved briefly after Naples and before St. Thomas. The guy called after Derek had moved to the Caribbean to tell him he was HIV-positive, so Derek was enraged and horrified, and he insisted that David come to St. Thomas to accompany him to an HIV test and explain how he could "do this" to him.

As was the case with most of the things Derek said and did, this made no sense. The only thing that was believable was the fear I could hear in his voice. AIDS is still a killer today, but in 1989, it was a death sentence. I was panicked too. He told me that David wasn't going to be there much longer, but that maybe I shouldn't come after all. I was devastated. If my gift copy of *Co-Dependent No More* had taught me nothing else, it was that I needed to forsake anything that had to do with my well-being, and that I needed to be by Derek's side during this trying and potentially life-threatening time. (I'm pretty sure that's what the book says—I never actually bothered to read it.) But Derek was adamant; he had his health to worry about, so he wanted me to stay away.

I spent the next two weeks hanging out with my friends Kurt and Tina, going out to the bars, and crashing at Kurt's condo. Everyone was asking me when I was leaving for St. Thomas. It was all I had been talking about all summer, and there had to be an explanation for my lobster glow. I was too embarrassed to tell them that the trip had been canceled, something most of them had predicted.

Then, after one particularly long night of partying, and with my summer-school finals behind me, I inexplicably found myself in the long-term-parking lot at Sky Harbor International Airport. I was wearing a pair of white shorts, a green Polo shirt, and blue Keds when I approached the Eastern Airlines ticket counter and asked for a one-way ticket to Charlotte Amalie.

"How many bags do you have to check, sir?" the bubbly blonde agent asked.

"None," I replied, which happened to be the exact amount of self-esteem I had left, too.

Moments later, we were 40,000 feet off the ground, with the captain letting us know about the glorious weather in St. Thomas.

If I was going to snap out of it and realize this "surprise" visit was misbegotten at best, it would have been at the airport in San Juan, where I was to get on a connecting flight. But by then, the adrenaline was unstoppable, and the thought of seeing Derek's face when I showed up in the lobby of the hotel had the anticipatory intensity of a dozen Christmas Eves.

After landing at the island's Fisher-Price airport, I quickly flew past the baggage carousel (singular), hopped in a rickety taxicab, and blurted out my destination.

"Stouffer Grand Beach Resort, please."

The ride was bumpy, but I sensed it would be nothing compared to what was next. The hotel was far less intimidating than I had imagined it to be, so I marched up to the front desk with no hesitation and said, "Do you know if Derek is working today?"

Before the attendant could say yes, I looked over my shoulder and there was Derek, his island glow immediately erased to a winter pale as he saw me.

"Kenneth," he said, in a tone that revealed he was equal parts happy and distressed to see me, a tone with which I was all too familiar.

"What are you doing here?" he asked, as he gave me a huge hug, all but lifting me off the ground. "It's so good to see you!"

In fact, *part* of him was very glad to see me. He managed to get the rest of the day off and loaded me and my lack of luggage into his trusty Mazda pickup truck. It seemed the resort had paid to have it ferried over, which I would soon learn was not the only fairy-themed item Derek still had with him from Florida.

The road home was a winding, narrow two-lane stretch, with near-death experiences waiting around every corner, and I'm not even counting the HIV. When we finally arrived at Derek's recently procured new "apartment," I was charmed to see that he was living in an actual treehouse. What was going on inside of it, however, would have made the Swiss Family Robinson dive back in the water and swim to New Guinea.

"Kenneth, I love you, and I'm so glad to see you. I'm so sorry I canceled your visit, but things have been extremely stressful for me since the whole AIDS test and everything," he said, as he pulled my shirt over my head and began to kiss me just inside the doorway. "I've been so scared and so lonely. I'm so glad you're here right now." Within moments, we were going at it like wild animals, the kind of breakup/make-up sex that you can have only with someone you truly despise.

When it was over, Derek revealed the full story. His HIV-positive "friend," David, had decided to stay in St. Thomas—surprise—and they were now treehouse "roommates." He pointed to the bedroll in the living room as proof that the relationship was platonic, but I was so satisfied with myself for having gotten him "back" for the afternoon that I didn't even care at that point. But a few hours later David came home from his job, and the real fun began.

After an initial attempt at being civil, the liquor started flowing, and David was in no mood to mince words.

"I knew you'd show up here," he sneered at me as he took a long drag of his cigarette, acting more like a bitter old queen than the twenty-year-old cutie he was. "I have to tell you, I was really intimidated when I heard about you, that you were this really smart guy and had accomplished all of these things," he continued, smoke coming out of his nostrils as he spoke. "But just look at you. You're pathetic. You're nothing."

I was speechless. I was twenty-two years old and chasing after the love of my life, and suddenly I was entwined in a scene from a Joseph L. Mankiewicz film, and I hadn't learned my lines.

A visibly stressed Derek broke it up, then offered to give me a tour of the island. He loaned me a bathing suit, and out the door we went. The beaches were spectacular, and as we floated in the warm, light blue water, I allowed myself to pretend that my fantasy month in the Caribbean was actually happening. But the dream was short-lived. Derek invited David to go out with us that night to what I learned was St. Thomas's only gay bar, a dive fittingly called Blues. (When you're in your early twenties, going to "the bar" was pretty much the only weekend activity there was, and this situation certainly warranted unbridled drinking.) As David and I shamelessly fought for Derek's attention, the bartender came over and announced that the man at the end of the bar wanted to buy "the cute guy in red" a drink. Derek, realizing that David and I both had red on hesitated, then asked the bartender, "Which of these cute guys?" The bartender pointed to me, a nice gesture that would end up being the final positive thing from the adventure.

As the drinks continued and the vicious tongues wagged, things got so ugly that Derek suggested I leave in the morning. I offered no resistance.

I was back less than forty-eight hours from when I left, $1,100 further in debt. My parents never even knew I had been gone.

I moved in with my friend Kurt for my final semester of college, and continued to pine for the love of my life. When I graduated that December, I had a job interview at the *Phoenix Gazette* lined up. I cockily thought I was a shoo-in. But when the job didn't pan out, I found that Phoenix, with its limited newspaper and publishing opportunities, wasn't exactly the ideal place for a recent journalism major to start a career.

I got an unexpected call from Derek one evening, telling me that he had moved back to Fort Lauderdale—without David—and that he was dying to see me. With no hesitation, I flew down for a visit. He told me how much he realized he missed me and hinted that he might be moving back to Phoenix soon. I tried not to get my hopes up again, but I returned home feeling cautiously optimistic that we were still destined to be together.

To make ends meet while I plotted my next move, a friend got me a good-paying job in the American Express call center she worked in, where I spent my days ignoring phone calls from clients while busily looking through the purchases of my favorite celebrities, including Debbie Harry and Madonna.

As I floundered, Derek made good on his promise, showing up in the early part of 1990. He got an apartment with his friend Dana, whom I had always loved.

Derek and I found ourselves in a new groove—seeing each other every day, going out to dinner and movies and bars—and the idea of staying in Phoenix, something I had never wanted to do, started to seem like a distinct possibility. We had been through a lot, but it seemed we had turned a corner and things were different now. He was older and finally ready to be serious, he said. And then along came Brian.

Brian was Dana's friend Kristen's kid brother. Kristen had a hunch that Brian might be gay, so Dana offered to spend some time with him, knowing that she had inadvertently turned into a fag hag now that Derek had moved in. By then I was spending nearly every night there, so I was half-kiddingly referred to as her "other roommate who doesn't pay rent." The second I laid eyes on him, I knew Brian was going to be trouble. He was nineteen and unbelievably cute, with blond hair and blue eyes, the exact type of surfer kid you would see in a Hollister ad today. Plus, he had that "straight" guy thing going on. But I sensed he was struggling with his sexuality and didn't want to be the jealous bitch in the gang, so I embraced him wholeheartedly. Because he was underage, I even let him use my old driver's license to get into the bars with us. (I had an extra because I had gotten a new one when I moved.)

And then it happened. Derek and Brian became involved, only this time the competition was much stiffer. It was a humbling experience at age twenty-two to feel you were old and washed-up, but Brian was that good-looking. I would see them together at our local nightclub, Preston's, and my heart would shatter. Thus began the ritual of the "fifth-drink cry," where I would be fun to be around until the fifth Jim Beam and 7 (Derek's drink of choice that had mysteriously become mine too) kicked in, and I would begin to sob uncontrollably. I was young and smart and cute enough—and plenty of guys were hitting on me—yet I felt like the Debbie Reynolds of Phoenix, crushed by losing her Eddie.

As pathetic as it sounds—and *pathetic* does not even do it justice—it's hard to explain how devastating losing him again was to me. Derek was more than a boyfriend. He represented the righting of a lifetime of wrongs, of oppression, of self-loathing, of feeling as if I would die alone or isolated from society. I was so damaged I was unable to see that the so-called solution was in many ways far worse than the initial problems. And even if that wasn't true, everyone was right: There were many other guys out there—just not for me yet.

I attempted some more self-esteem-eroding antics— stacking up the patio furniture by the pool at Derek and Dana's complex to try to peer into the second-floor window, lurking in the bushes—but to no avail. Derek called the cops on me, and I was pulled over just after I wrapped up stalking for the night. (I was leaving anyway; why'd he have to call them?) The female police officer asked me where I had been, and I admitted everything, but in gender-unspecific terms.

When the dispatch people informed her that "the gentleman" did not wish to press charges, the policewoman looked at me in complete horror, and simply said, "You can go."

And with that I was finally done. It took that grave indignity—of nearly being arrested at six in the morning for lurking outside my "true love's" apartment—for me to finally see how messed up I had become. I moved to Los Angeles a month later, and the Derek drama was finally put to rest.

As the years passed, Derek and I actually became friends. We always had fun together, so it made sense. His mother's suicide was a turning point, and I watched him struggle through some dark times in his life. But for many years now, Derek has found stability in his personal and professional life, working as a funeral director. It's crazy, but after going back to school to become a variety of things—a hair stylist, a pilot, a candlestick maker—it was this *Six Feet Under*-inspired move that stuck.

A few years ago, Derek contacted me with some serious news. He said he had just cremated a thirtysomething-year-old man who died of AIDS, his body withered away to just 105 pounds. If Derek had been shaken by the fact that the man was younger than he was—yet had still succumbed to a disease in a way that we think rarely happens in this day and age—he was even more shaken when he realized the man was Brian. Coincidentally, it turned out Brian was a friend of the owner of the funeral home where Derek worked and had actually done some graphic design work for the place, designing the company's logo. Derek found out that Brian had endured two failed marriages before finally fully accepting that he was gay. Although I know none of the specifics, I do know that there's nothing like self-hatred to make you do risky things. It had been twenty years since this impossibly beautiful creature put the nail in my dream's coffin, and now Derek had put him in his. It was a sobering moment.

dead ringers society

I was coming out of Café D'Etoile on Santa Monica Boulevard in West Hollywood one night when I was first asked the question: "Are you that guy from *Dead Poets Society*?"

The inquisitor was a handsome dark-haired guy in his mid-twenties who smiled as he stopped me, his two friends looking on from their table, clearly impressed by his boldness.

The movie had come out the previous summer, and while it was a smash, none of the young actors in it were household names yet, so I wasn't even sure which guy he was referring to. I had seen the film and developed an instant crush on Robert Sean Leonard, but then later realized people weren't talking about him when my friend Mark's sister Lois mentioned to him that the "shy kid" in the *Dead Poets Society* looked "just like Kenny." This, of course, turned out to be Ethan Hawke. That I managed to be disappointed by the comparison—Robert Sean Leonard was the *hot* one!—would come back to haunt me, as I learned that your ego is the thing that bruises easiest as you grow older.

After that first incident in the restaurant, the whole thing kind of exploded. I was living in Los Angeles now, and tourists would come up to me all the time and ask me if I had been in *Dead Poets Society*. Even when I said no, sometimes young girls would ask for photos. I would hear whispers at every party I went to. Guys would be pointing at me in bars.

It was around this time I first met Sean, when he tried to pick me up outside the Greenwich Village Pizzeria in West

Hollywood. I had barely been in California a month when Sean pulled me into the restaurant's restroom and shared a bump of coke with me, then asked me if I wanted to come home with him. I was intrigued—his blond hair and angular face were almost as eye-grabbing as his muscular physique and fully-inked arms—but I was with a friend visiting from back home, so I just laughed his invitation off wondering who this tattooed love boy thought he was to be so forward. I would later find out.

Truth be told, I was scared of him. But as the months went by, we'd keep running into each other at bars and parties, and eventually I had to admit that I wanted to know what he was all about. I'd never met anyone like him before—so quiet and mysterious—like James Dean's older brother on steroids. I was completely besotted.

I experienced many of my "firsts" with Sean—my first ride on the back of a Harley being one of the safer activities he introduced me to. I had stayed overnight at his converted-garage apartment near the Beverly Center, and he loaned me a Mr. Bubble T-shirt to wear before we headed out on the road the following afternoon. (That must have been a sight.) Everywhere we'd go there was a buzz surrounding Sean, and people rarely thought I was "somebody" in his presence. He wasn't a movie star or anything, but you'd never know it the way people fell over when he walked into a room.

And what felt great is that he seemed equally infatuated with me.

"You know what I love about your body?" he said to me of my now-beefy 138-pound frame when we were in the shower one day.

"No, what?" I asked, embarrassed to be naked next to his muscular body.

"Your arm is the same size here as it is here," he said, placing his powerful right hand around my bicep and then my wrist.

He seemed to be every guy in L.A.'s idea of a dream, but you didn't have to be an interventionist to realize Sean had a serious drug problem. And nearly every time we got together, we wound up getting high—usually on crystal meth, his drug of choice. In 1990, though, crystal meth wasn't associated with the destructive "party and play" lifestyle in which it became a central player once the Internet era dawned. (And unlike my father, I was born without the addiction gene and could sample anything and never think about it again.) Crystal, as we called it, was just speed. You'd snort it—it burned a lot, like Drain-O—and then you'd stay up for days. But this was pre-Viagra, so we weren't having sex or doing anything "unsafe"—well, nothing unsafe besides putting toxic chemicals cooked up in some toothless stranger's bathtub in our systems. In fact, you physically couldn't have sex on this stuff. We would just stay up and talk and talk and talk. I have never tripped on acid or mushrooms or done LSD, but the crystal method struck me as similar to the way people have described the experience. Things come into focus. What's really important becomes much clearer. If you're lucky, your apartment might even wind up spotless. Even better, it was when Sean was high that he would let the wall down just a bit and reveal little things about himself, about his childhood, and about his feelings for me.

The affair was short-lived—as I tried to get closer to him, he pushed me away—and it was clear his incredible beauty had left him feeling exploited and angry. It was only years later that I learned that he had posed for some famous photographers and had been featured in some notable works of art.

But as brief as our liaison was, the fact was he entered my life at a moment when I needed someone to make me feel attractive and special again, after several years of having my self-worth raked over the coals, even if I can now admit I was perhaps as much a volunteer as a victim in that outing.

With or without Sean, Hollywood was electric in those days, and every night was a whole new adventure. One evening my friends and I would be at the birthday party *Interview* magazine was throwing for Robert Downey, Jr., and the next night we'd be playing pool at the Hollywood Athletic Club. Weekends we would be out drinking at all the bars in West Hollywood, then dancing until the sun came up at Probe before hitting the Del Taco drive-through. The Sunset Strip was a cesspool of celebrities and drugs—River Phoenix's dead body was a sad souvenir of that time—and we couldn't get enough. We were young and reasonably cute, but sometimes it seemed there was something more to the special way we were being treated.

I must admit, I worked that mistaken identity pretty hard, even if I stopped short of lying outright. It was much easier getting into clubs and parties in Los Angeles when people thought you were "someone," even if they weren't sure exactly who that someone was.

Years later, I discovered my "twin" Ethan Hawke lived around the corner from my apartment in New York. Although I've resisted, I've always wanted to ask him if he ever was confronted about his "secret gay past." Hollywood heartthrobs are frequently the subject of gay rumors—true or false—and it seems nearly impossible that someone wouldn't have asked him at some point about his wild West Hollywood "phase."

This went on for a couple of years, and it was the beginning of a lifetime of playing "You know who you look like?"

By the mid-'90s, Ethan Hawke was well-known, and no one was asking me if I was "that kid" in *Dead Poets Society* anymore. Instead, people were occasionally telling me I looked like Cameron from *Ferris Bueller's Day Off*—the ultimate answer to the question: Why the long face? Fortunately, Cameron was replaced in the late '90s and early '00s when I started to get Ben Affleck quite a bit (mostly from straight men), which I ate up—I thought he was way better-looking than Ethan—even though I knew it was really my goatee that was getting all the attention.

But then around the time I hit my mid-thirties, things (or I?) really started to get ugly.

In the summer of 2001, I was having lunch at the Howard Johnson's in Times Square with my visiting brother (Terence) and sister (Jennifer) when a swarthy waiter approached our table. He was so excited that before he could even take our order, he told us we would never guess which movie star had just been in there. Charmed by how enthusiastic he was, we took the bait and asked, "Who?" Beaming, he told us he had waited on John Travolta, then proceeded to tell us all about the encounter, from what Travolta ordered to who he was with. We smiled and acted thoroughly impressed. Then he got distracted and looked directly at me and said, "Speaking of movie stars, you know who *you* look just like?" Flushed with pride in front of my siblings and expecting one of the flattering comparisons I'd gotten over the years—while secretly praying for just one James Van Der Beek (shouldn't our mutual huge foreheads garner at least one comparison in my lifetime?)—I leaned back, practically batting my eye lashes, and said, "Who?"

"Denis Leary," he replied, clearly proud of himself for his astute observational abilities. My sister immediately pointed and laughed at me, while Terence covered his mouth to hide his laughter as I turned bright red.

It didn't matter how many people later insisted that they thought Leary was "handsome"; the damage to my ego had been done. Handsome or not, a gruff, chain-smoking actor ten years my senior was hardly a comparison I was ready to deal with. And why would a waiter in Times Square in 2001 know who Denis Leary was *anyway*?

Things have been relatively quiet since I turned forty, other than the occasional Janko Tipsarevic, who is a Serbian tennis player with facial hair, and even a few Ben Afflecks again once he grew a beard for *Argo*. Still feeling *leery* of comparisons, I found some comfort in hearing that one of my best friends who used to get told he looked like Kevin Bacon now gets William H. Macy—and that another who was often literally mistaken for rocker Bryan Adams now gets Philip

Seymour Hoffman. When I was really down, I'd recall that my old roommate James used to get mistaken for Tom Arnold—and this happened when James was in his early twenties!

Recently, though, just when it seemed my doppelgänger days were behind me, I was thrown a kick serve by one of the South American coaches at a tennis camp I attended in upstate New York with my brother. The instructor kept staring at me, but I wasn't sure if he was admiring my wicked slice backhand, or if he was just concerned that I might pass out. (I have a tendency to turn *really* red when I play tennis.) It turned out it was neither.

When we both finally wound up in the same rest area at the same time, he came up to me and said, "You know who you look just like?"

All too familiar with the drill, I paused and said, "No, who?"

"Andres Nocioni," he replied, with a big smile. The seeming compliment landed like a volley in the bottom of the net; no one recognized the name. He quickly explained that Nocioni was an Argentine basketball player for the Chicago Bulls. Now, despite my newly acquired third-degree sunburn/tan—my version of "swarthy"—I still couldn't fathom how I could look like an Argentine. But then he told me that Nocioni has "the light hair and the blue eyes, just like you." And another one of the instructors from South America backed him up.

Although I was exhausted from another eight-hour day on the court, my curiosity was still strong enough for me to look up my latest doppelgänger on the Web when I got back to my cabin. I still didn't really see the resemblance—Nocioni looked more like Shaggy from *Scooby Doo* to me—but I was willing to cut the coach some slack. First of all, Nocioni is a good dozen years younger than I am, and a professional athlete at that. More important, though, Coach never mentioned the name Denis Leary.

the porn identity

It was Los Angeles, 1991. I had never been to a roommate service before, yet I could still sense that the scene in front of me was not the industry norm. The place reeked of Drakkar Noir, and everyone seemed oddly overdressed for a Thursday afternoon.

It was pre-Craigslist, so after failing to land a word-of-mouth apartment and striking out with the listings in the back of *Frontiers* and *Edge,* West Hollywood's two free gay rags, I decided to take a chance.

Roommate Matchers had a huge office on the corner of Fairfax and Beverly Boulevard, and although it was ostensibly in business to hook people up with housing accommodations, its reputation extended beyond that.

Knowing what I did about the place, I felt obligated to visit the tanning salon, get my highlights touched up, and cram in a last-minute workout at the Sports Connection—known around West Hollywood as the Sports Erection—before my afternoon appointment with my "roommate matcher." Never mind your credit rating, everyone knows that flaxen locks and a healthy glow are requirements for getting approved for a new apartment, at least in L.A. Then I put on my best Polo oxford, denim shorts, and blue Keds, and headed over.

After filling out some paperwork, I met my matcher, who interviewed me about my likes, dislikes, and living habits before having me pose for a photograph for their Book of Matches. Chuck Woolery could not have done a better job.

Once my profile was in the Men Seeking Men "system"—which in 1991 amounted to a loose-leaf binder with Polaroids stapled to hand-written profiles encased in plastic—I was free to flip through the books of guys looking for roommates, as well as people with rooms for rent.

Since I had never gotten around to buying any furniture for my previous pad, moving into an existing setup was starting to look like the way to go, so I sat down on the sofa with the "rooms for rent" book and dug in.

I don't think I had flipped through more than a dozen "profiles" before I came across this listing:

"Room for Rent in West Hollywood Bungalow. $500/month, utilities included."

The location was perfect—on North Croft Avenue in the heart of Boys' Town—and the rent was right. But the real draw was the photo ... of potential roommates Dennis and Ken. I don't remember if it was stated or not, but it looked as if they were a couple. I found myself hoping they were not. Both were all-American types in their twenties, with dark hair and military haircuts. But where Dennis was a little hefty and average-looking, Ken was athletic and sexy, with a devilish look in his eye that assured you he was trouble—in the best possible way.

I drove home and immediately called to inquire. The guy on the phone had a deep, masculine voice that matched the photo to a T, and while I wasn't sure which guy it was, my gut—and crotch—told me I was speaking with Ken. After going over the logistics of the deal—yes, it was still available; the new roommate could move in on the first; you didn't have to sign a lease, but a one-month deposit was required—my potential new roommate informed me that I could come look at it the next day. And then things became more personal.

"So, what do you look like?" he asked, as if this were the most normal of roommate-interview questions.

"What kind of guys do you like?" he then wanted to know.

A few more questions followed before there was something else on his mind.

"Are you getting *hard* right now?"

I was—I'd been staring at Ken in the Polaroid as we chatted on the phone—and the next thing I knew, I had ejaculated with a total stranger on the phone. (This alone costs a straight guy $3.99 for the first minute and 99 cents for each additional minute.) Although I had agreed to come see the place the following evening, I was mortified by what had happened—I was a nice boy from Michizona, I reminded myself—and had decided I was too embarrassed to show my face on Croft Avenue. But after a second trip to Roommate Matchers failed to produce any promising leads, let alone complimentary phone sex, I drove over to Dennis and Ken's place to see what else they had to offer.

The house turned out to be an adorable duplex on a quiet, tree-lined street with a view of the Hollywood Hills just to the north and the actual street called Melrose Place to the south. An elderly couple lived next door, and Dennis and Ken were just like their photo: young and very friendly. They were indeed a couple and had met in the military. The bungalow was exactly the type of place I had dreamed of living in when I first moved to Southern California.

After some small talk and a quick tour of the common areas—a beautiful living room and dining room with hardwood floors, plus a retro-looking kitchen with pink countertops and '50s appliances—Dennis, who it was clear was the decision maker of the duo, took me down the long hallway to the bedroom that would be mine. It was a good-sized space that would more than accommodate my meager belongings, and when we got inside, he made some sheepish comment about having had fun talking to me the night before. While I was relieved the elephant in the room had been addressed, I was disappointed to realize I had jerked off with the *wrong* elephant. I wasn't exactly naïve at this point, so I wasn't sure if going into this new living arrangement with a "sexual secret" with one roommate was a wise decision. But the house seemed perfect, so I was willing to look past it if he was. I moved in about two weeks later.

Life in West Hollywood started out great. I quickly became a fixture at Rage and Revolver, my two favorite bars on Santa Monica Boulevard, and my old roommate James and I started hanging out together again, after a bit of a hiccup when we went our separate ways after living together on Bundy. He even introduced me to a guy who played tennis, Marc. (I had barely played since leaving Arizona.) I was excited.

Things at home were coming together, more or less. Dennis, I was finding, was a control freak, always trying to get Ken and me to take a more active role in the upkeep of the house. Each Sunday evening, Dennis would leave a list of chores on a dry-erase board by the telephone stand, which had the unintentional effect of bringing Ken and me closer, mocking Dennis's mother-hen ways. Ken was studying math at UCLA in his post-military life, so he would always be at his living-room desk getting stoned while doing his homework. I was kind of sweet on him—everything he did seemed to come so effortlessly to him—but I also saw him as a big brother. In me, I think he recognized a kid trying to find his place in the world. We were only a few years apart in age, but the difference between 24 and 28 is huge in a young man's life. We would frequently stay up talking and laughing all night, often prompting Dennis—aka "Dad"—to come out and scream at us to "Keep it down!" That, naturally, made us all the more hysterical.

One afternoon, James and I were out shopping when we popped into the local sex shop, Drake's. We were checking out the videos and then flipping through the latest issues of *Honcho* and *Torso* when I suddenly saw a face that looked very familiar.

"James," I said, almost panicked. "Get over here."

"What?" he said, annoyed to be pulled away from the latest Falcon title.

I pointed to a photo of a man grunting as he took Lex Baldwin's thick cock up his ass in the back of an eighteen-wheeler.

"That's the exact same face Ken made when I asked him how he thought Dennis would take the news that I was going to be late with this month's rent," I said.

James looked and then took a step back, as if he might fall down.

"Oh, my God!" he said, covering his mouth and his eyes tripled in size. "You're living with Mike Henson!"

It was as if he had just found out Madonna had been my babysitter when I was growing up.

Mike Henson, he explained, was one of the biggest porn stars of the late '80s, having starred in William Higgins's classic 1987 *Top Gun* parody, *Big Guns*.

And just like that, a lot of things made more sense. Why Dennis had been so determined to put his sexual "mark" on me first, during our initial interaction ... on the phone. Why people seemed to be whispering about Ken everywhere we'd go. (He was cute, but the kind of buzz Ken generated went beyond that.) And why Ken was so irresistibly appealing in that initial Roommate Matchers ad—he was a professional "model"!

James and I reeled most of the afternoon. It was a great story, but I began to wonder what I should "do" with the information. Should I say something about it to them? Should I just leave things as they were? Had they thought I knew all along—and maybe wanted to move in because of it?

But it didn't seem to be relevant at this point; "Mike" had become a full-time college student.

And that's when the strangest thing happened. I was off work that day, so I came home from hanging out with James around 4 p.m. Dennis was still at work and Ken was in class when I entered through the side door into the kitchen and noticed something spread out on the dining-room table: black-and-white nudes of my roommate Ken, from one edge of the table to the other. I was startled. There was no way they could have known that I had just found out about Ken's other life, yet somehow they coincidentally just happened to let the information—which had never been mentioned once up until this point—"slip" on that exact same day? I had chills.

I retreated to my room, but later that evening, the guys asked me if I wanted to join them for Mexican food with some friends in Silverlake. We hadn't socialized outside of the house much, but I immediately said yes, and invited James along for the ride. It became clear that they had left the photos out to start a discussion, because that was all we talked about over dinner. Although I had never heard of Mike Henson, I was an enormous fan of one of his porn peers and (I came to find out) *Big Guns* costars, Johnny Davenport, so when Ken told me that they were friends and gave me the lowdown on my dream man, it was like being at the hottest high school reunion of all time. As the margaritas continued flowing, Dennis, Ken, James, and I found ourselves back at the ranch. Gay chat lines were de rigueur at the time, so somehow Ken and I ended up calling one as we continued talking about his porn past. We were using the phone in the living room, but when we got a hot-sounding guy on the other end, I gave him my personal number, and then the phone rang way down the hall.

Ken and I went running into my bedroom to answer, but within a few seconds we had forgotten about the phone. I was equal parts titillated and terrified. Here was this legendary porn star drunk and flirty and in my bedroom while his boyfriend was with my blond buddy in the living room. The script for the evening had been written for us—and it was one Mike Henson was all too familiar with. The majority of me wanted to devour "Mike" alive—I hadn't allowed myself to be sexually free since my split with Derek (the Sean thing was more psychological than physical)—but this was 1992, and all I could think was that there was absolutely no way the star of *Big Guns* didn't have HIV. Sure, I knew about safe sex. But having safe sex with someone who you thought didn't have

HIV was entirely different from having it with someone who you believed did. But the moment had arrived, and I had to decide, so I compromised. A few well-placed kisses and lick of his chest and groin devolved into my giving him a hand job that both my diary and an Evangelical Christian prom queen could be proud of.

Pleased that I had had my (not-as-big-as-it-might-have-been) moment with Mike Henson, life returned to normal for a while. My friend Carolyn had moved back to town, so I was enjoying spending time with her again. She, James, and Marc took me to my favorite Mexican restaurant in West Hollywood to celebrate my twenty-fifth birthday that June, a night that was fun until one too many margaritas led me to drunk-dial Derek back in Scottsdale, who by now was living with yet another new boyfriend.

But then Dennis became ill—spending entire nights awake hacking uncontrollably—and I became terrified. I cared about these two and wasn't sure what was going to happen from one day to the next. They never talked to me about their health. And even though I wasn't scared of "catching" anything—well, I guess I was scared enough to chicken out on a romp in the sack with the star of *Big Guns*—I felt alone and alienated from the grim reality of it all.

Feeling helpless about the epidemic swirling around me, I volunteered at AIDS Project Los Angeles, where I became an "AIDS buddy," getting together each week with a terminally ill guy named Joseph in Hollywood proper. Each week, we'd watch *Beverly Hills, 90210* together and argue about who was cuter: Brandon or Dylan. (Brandon, obviously.)

I know the mere mention of AIDS made my mom terrified—what mother wouldn't be, not really understanding what her young son was up to in those days?—but when I told her about my new volunteer work, she said what was probably the kindest thing she's ever said to me.

"Well, I think that's really nice," she told me on the

phone one evening. "I know if I were ever terminally ill, I can't think of anyone I would rather spend time with." My heart was glowing.

Things turned dark that winter when I caught the flu for the first time in my life. I had never known what "influenza" was—I thought it just meant a really bad cold—but I found out that December when I had to make the harrowing decision between shitting or vomiting on the bathroom floor. I honestly thought I was going to die. I must have had a really high fever, because after the bathroom incident I wound up in bed, where I "dreamt" I could not fall asleep for what felt like days. It was an excruciating hallucination that I will never forget. I was sweating uncontrollably yet freezing, so I sat in a ball next to the space heater my mom had bought me when she found out during a particularly cold winter that our bungalow did not have central heating.

And then it happened, as if he were auditioning for the "Here's Johnny!" scene in *The Shining*.

Dennis, looking as out of his mind as I felt, came barreling into my bedroom in the middle of the night, screaming, "Do you have any idea how much this heater costs to run?" (He was clearly regretting the "utilities included" part of my rental agreement.) I didn't even know if this was actually happening or was part of the dream, let alone how much money I was "wasting."

He then became increasingly aggressive and abusive, listing everything I had ever done that had ever bothered him, from the way I washed silverware to the way I spent so much time in my room instead of "socializing" with him and Ken. Then he rattled off the endless ways in which I was the most selfish person on God's green earth.

"Kenneth only thinks of three people: Kenneth, Kenneth, and Kenneth."

I may have been delirious, but I was cognizant enough to know I had to get out of there. I already felt as if I were about to die, and now I feared I might be killed instead.

114

Compounding matters, I suddenly felt as if I had no friends to turn to. Just as it seemed my friendship with James was back on track, he had grown jealous of my friendship with Marc and stopped speaking to me again. And perhaps out of loyalty to his original friend, Marc now seemed to be following James's lead. It was an all-time low.

The only person I seemed to have on my side was a guy who lived in my old complex, who despite being mentally disabled (or as a result of being?) had developed an enormous crush on me. It all started out sweet. Amir was the landlord's younger brother, and though he was slow, he was kind-hearted and was always up for a late-night chat. Because I knew he was *slow*, it never entered my mind that he might be gay. (It had been a long time since I had seen Shaun Cassidy play a mentally challenged romantic in the made-for-TV movie *Like Normal People*.) Amir seemed harmless enough. But when he found out I was moving, he began to shower me with flowers and presents, and I started to become a little uncomfortable. After I left, he called me repeatedly—and started mailing me a series of love letters—so I reluctantly agreed to meet him for dinner one night, with the intention of letting him know that we probably wouldn't be seeing each other very often now that I had moved from the Bundy to West Hollywood. Amir showed up at the designated restaurant, Pennyfeathers on La Cienega, in a taxi—further proof that he was mentally disabled—and the conversation was repeatedly interrupted by porn star Ryan Idol, who was sitting at the table next to us queening it up and demanding everyone's attention. Although Amir seemed to understand what I was saying, he later began showing up at every bar I had ever told him I frequented, dressed in elaborate disguises: wigs, hats, glasses, ascots—anything he could dream up. (A mentally capable CIA agent couldn't have done it better.) The whole thing reached a breaking point when I realized he was following me home one night as I left Rage.

After this unsettling series of events, I finally decided it was time to leave Los Angeles behind and pursue my true love. Only moving to New York City was still too lofty a goal for this weary twenty-five-year-old. Instead, I would move to Washington, D.C., to be closer to my brothers, and to try to figure out what it was I wanted to be when I grew up.

Nursing my body as I nursed my emotional wounds, I informed Dennis that I would be moving out that weekend. As far as I was concerned, he forfeited his right to thirty days' notice when he made me feel unsafe in my own bed. Ken stayed quiet, but he gave me a look that said he was sorry it had come to this. I would crash at my friend Carolyn's loft in Little Tokyo before flying to Washington at the end of the month.

The day after I told Dennis I was leaving, the transmission on my Volkswagen mysteriously fell out on the 5 freeway. The garage where I had it towed said my car had none of the necessary fluids it should have had—a week after I had had it serviced at a Jiffy Lube—leading me to the inescapable conclusion that someone close to home was likely responsible for this act of sabotage. Things couldn't possibly get any worse than they were at that moment, I thought. And while Washington was hardly New York City, I was tired of being jerked around—even in the home of a popular porn professional.

love allergy

After three up-and-down years living in Los Angeles, I had come east with a different mindset, determined to make more friends and be more open to the prospect of falling in love again. And sure enough, it worked. I first met Rafael in a basement bar in Washington on 17th Street Northwest called Trumpet's. I had gone there with Keith, a friend from my internship on Capitol Hill, and Rafael and I ended up being introduced through mutual friends.

He was truly tall, dark, and handsome, with an accent and name to back up the cliché. I was instantly infatuated. He told me he was originally from Bogotá, Colombia, but he went to college in Florida and now lived just outside the city, in Arlington, Virginia. I knew Arlington well, as my parents were living there when my oldest brother was born and subsequently died of crib death. Because of my father's service in the Korean War, Kevin was buried in Arlington National Cemetery.

Rafael and I exchanged phone numbers. He gave me a kiss on the cheek—how Continental, as my mom would say— and we parted ways. Still buzzing from the cheap vodka-and-cranberries (or Cape Cods, as they were known in Washington), I walked home to my efficiency apartment just around the corner, on 16th Street Northwest, and let both my head and my heart dream. I pulled out the napkin with Rafael's number on it and dialed, curious to hear his voice once more before going to bed. Cell phones and caller ID were rare to nonexistent, so I felt confident that I would get his answering machine. I dialed. It rang once, and then again. Then there he was: "Hello?"

Click.

I felt my face turn beet red, alone in my tiny home. I was mortified. How could he possibly be home already, I thought. He lived *across* the river. I walked away from the phone stand and tried to pretend it hadn't happened when my phone suddenly rang. With flashbacks to my babysitting days and Carol Kane in *When a Stranger Calls*—"The call is coming from *inside* the house. Get out of the house!"—I stood up in horror and waited for what felt like fifteen minutes while the phone rang five times before my answering machine's outgoing greeting played, the beep sounded, and I heard his voice:

"*Hola, guapo.* It's me, Rafael. Just wanted to say that it was great meeting you tonight. I'm looking forward to seeing you again soon. Sleep tight, and I will talk to you soon. Good night."

And that's how it all began, what my friends dubbed a "star-sixty-nine romance." Rafa and I fell hard for each other, and we became inseparable. I had set out to make more friends in my new life, but this plan quickly unraveled. Every nonworking moment was spent with Rafael. Soon my apartment acted as the city's most expensive storage unit. Although Arlington was a return to the suburbs, Rafael lived in a beautiful three-story town house, and with him in it, it was becoming a home.

About nine months later, he decided to buy his first place, a spacious one-bedroom in a high-rise near the Arlington Courthouse with spectacular views of the city, and asked me to make it official and move in with him. I accepted. Soon, my parents and sister met my new guy on their Thanksgiving trip to Washington, and we followed it up with a visit to Arizona. What a difference a year makes.

It was the morning of our one-year anniversary that Rafael made the brave decision to wake me up at 7:30. I make it a point not to get up before noon, so right away I knew he was up to something big.

Rafael explained he had a surprise for me and that we needed to be somewhere by eight o'clock. I threw on some clothes and pretended to be a good sport.

I slept through the ride, but I woke up as we pulled off of North Capitol Street into the parking lot of the Washington Animal Rescue League. Rafael explained that after seeing me with my family cat over the holidays in Arizona, he wanted to adopt a kitten for me as my anniversary present. In order to have the best selection, we had to be the first ones there when adoption hours began. I was stunned and touched. He was right: I missed Tweet horribly, but I could hardly move him, being the lizard-killing desert feline that he was, into a high-rise in the city. Rafael had picked just the right gift. It cemented all the feelings I had about him—and reassured me that moving in with him was the right decision.

The second we walked in the door, a little black, white, and orange kitten demanded our attention. He and his four siblings, along with their stray-cat mom, were on display in the Pet of the Week window. Since I'd grown up with Siamese cats, my first instinct was to go for the gray brother, but this other guy was having none of it. He took his little paw and pounded on the glass one more time, just to make sure we'd seen him. We had, and it wasn't long before we had him in a cardboard cat carrier in the backseat of the car. This kitten was just begging us to get him out of there, and that little pink nose was too much for me to refuse. I was in love. On the ride home, Rafael and I threw a bunch of names around until I blurted out Troy—in the quick, high-pitch way we'd call Tweet—and the name just seemed right.

Troy was the perfect kitten: fun, fearless, and always in the mood to play. Our apartment was on the twelfth floor and had a small balcony. Troy loved to scare the hell out of me by walking along the ledge, all the while surveying the birds flying nearby, sometimes standing on his hind legs to stand up to swing at them. Occasionally he'd wander off to the neighbors' balconies, and they'd freak out wondering how this cat had suddenly appeared. I'd always loved those hidden-camera shows and thought his high jinks were adorable.

But as my love affair with Troy was growing, my relationship with Rafael was becoming more complicated.

Once the honeymoon was over, a few things became apparent. Although we shared similar values and wanted the same things in life, we had few mutual interests. He loved hanging out with his Latin friends in bars till closing time, speaking Spanish and telling what he and his friends described as "jokes." He and his Latino friends seemed inordinately amused by the sight of a grown man wearing a tie that was too short. (It was particularly hilarious if it was worn while riding around on a tricycle.) Forget about *The Late Show With David Letterman*; *Sabado Gigante* was *it*. ("That Don Francisco is so funny!") I was more selective about my friends (speaking the same language wasn't my only criteria) and enjoyed a more subtle type of humor. Troy understood these things about me. Like me, Troy was selective about whose lap he sat on. And Troy never got up before noon, either. Troy was *always* in the mood to watch old *Bob Newhart* and *Mary Tyler Moore* reruns. And he would *never* complain when I'd watch the same Woody Allen movie for the hundredth time. Troy would even indulge me when I wanted to watch Woody's depressing Bergman period, and only slept through part of *Interiors*. Rafael, on the other hand, would be snoring within five minutes of anything I picked out at the video store.

But despite our differences, my boyfriend and I loved each other and were committed to making our relationship work. We enjoyed riding bikes, cooking dinner, and playing cards together, and his way with English as a Second Language always made me smile. (There's something about a grown man ordering a "squirrel" margarita at a Mexican restaurant—that's half lime, half raspberry, also known as a "swirl"—and talking about a "Muppet" show at his niece's birthday party that I found irresistible. (For the uninitiated, all Muppets are puppets, but not all puppets are Muppets.) And we'd spend holidays with my family in Washington or Arizona and vacation in Colombia on the off times when members of his family weren't staying with us for three months at a stretch.

Then, about four years into the relationship—and three years after we adopted Troy—Rafael started to get sick all the time. He was always sneezing and seemed to have an every-season postnasal drip. This went on for nearly a year until a doctor friend of Rafael's suggested that he was likely allergic to something. The friend even said that it was possible that someone could develop an allergy ... like to cats.

Well, without even consulting an allergist, Rafael became certain that Troy was the root of his health problems. He said that he thought we should start trying to find Troy a new home. I wasn't as convinced—on either count. And I found myself becoming increasingly less sympathetic about Rafael's "health problems."

You're *making yourself* cough, I'd think to myself, sounding frighteningly similar to my mother. Or I'd mumble, "Don't be such a baby" and then deny I'd said anything when he reacted.

Because Rafael was self-employed, he had to pay for his visits to the doctor. I saw this as an excuse for him to get out of being properly tested, so I offered to foot the bill for him to see an allergist. He finally acquiesced, and much to my dismay, the results came back quickly and definitively: Rafael tested "highly allergic" to cats. Although this could hardly be perceived as personal, to me somehow it was. The lab might as well have said he'd tested highly allergic to *me.*

I was torn. I loved Rafael dearly, but I loved my little critter, too. I was beside myself. Rafael thought this meant that it was time for me to give in, but I was still scrambling for other options. The doctors prescribed Claritin-D (useless), suggested we get an air filter (useless and expensive), and suggested we keep Troy out of our bedroom (heartbreaking). Every night for the previous three years, Troy had slept on my pillow, with his furry little body partially draped over my head. I loved having his little pink-nosed face staring down at me and hearing him purr at night. When Rafael and I started to close the bedroom door at night, Troy was upset and confused. (I, of course, was beyond distraught.) He would cry outside the door for hours, and I'd end up sneaking out to the sofa to sleep with him.

Rafael's allergies just seemed to get worse. Finally he sat me down and said that he had given everything a try, but that he didn't think he could live with a cat any longer. Rafael wanted to know one thing: "Is it going to be him or me?"

It was at this moment that I had to be completely honest about the state of my life—and my relationship. I loved Rafael. And I loved Troy. But I asked myself, Will Rafael be around in ten years? And I asked myself if Troy would. More than anything, I asked myself, Which one of them couldn't I bear to be without?

Troy and I moved into a new apartment in Dupont Circle about a month later. He was scared at first—and we didn't have a balcony for him to dangle off of—but he could still sleep on my head at night, and he adjusted.

To avoid acknowledging what was really going on, Rafael and I continued to see each other regularly for another three months or so. You know, "I *just* got a new place 'cause he was allergic to cats." But by the beginning of the New Year, he said he was thinking about moving back to Bogotá. We talked about my going along, but we both knew it wasn't going to happen. He moved a few months later, and Troy and I headed for New York City. Troy was scared of moving again. But unlike Rafael, he supported my desire to take a crack at the Big Apple, something that had been an increasingly contentious topic between us.

Troy lived to be thirteen and became far too big to sleep on my head. But there wasn't a morning that went by when I didn't wake up—with one of his big white feet in my face—very happy with my decision.

It wasn't until a few years after the move that I met someone I really fell for again. When Michael and I first started to get serious, he would sometimes get jealous of Troy, and accuse me of "loving Troy" more than I loved him. Of course I'd tell him that this was ridiculous: The love you have for a pet and the love you have for a romantic partner are entirely different things.

Unlike with Rafael, Michael and I have chosen not to move in together, and I'm more than happy with this arrangement. Although we have been together more than twice as long as Rafael and I were and there are no signs of an impending cat allergy, I still would never want to have to make that decision again. I knew how much Troy hated it when we moved—and I suspect my replacement cat, Larry, might just feel the same way.

dad, interrupted

Sometimes it's hard even for me to believe that what happened with my dad actually occurred. Not seeing or hearing anything about your own father for twenty years just doesn't happen to real people. It only happens in movies, in soap operas, and to crazy guests on talk shows. And no real-life father reverts at age forty into a nonfunctioning, childlike creature.

Dad was what I like to think of as a "classic" alcoholic—a kinder way of saying fun and genial when he was sober, mean and abusive when he was drunk—who had increasing trouble holding down a job as his years of drinking took their toll.

My mom was just seventeen and Dad was twenty-six when she became pregnant, so they did what people did in the late '50s. They got married and settled down, first in an apartment in Arlington, Virginia, just across the river from the supermarket where they had met in Takoma Park, Maryland, where Dad worked with Mom's older sister, Dianne. Mom used to visit Dianne at the snack bar when she was on duty, and Dad eventually made his move at the urging of a relative who had noticed how cute Molly was. When their child, a son my mom named Kevin, inexplicably died two months later—of what is called SIDS now but was known as "crib death" then—my mom's already disapproving mother told her on the ride to the cemetery that now she could "divorce the bum" and put this mistake behind her. But the loss of their child had brought my parents closer together. Mom instead opted to put her heartless mother behind her—and soon there were three more Walsh boys.

But over the years it became apparent that, as much as my mom didn't want to admit it, her mother was right. My dad would be good for a while, and then his twin brother, Kenny, would blow into town, and the cycle would start all over again. Drinking until they passed out. Not showing up for work. Calling his boss when he was drunk off his ass and making crazed threats. Dad and Kenny were born very prematurely when premature babies rarely survived, and the fact that they were even alive was considered a miracle by everyone who'd known them as babies. Perhaps that had something to do with their unshakable bond, which Mom says went so far as to include Kenny trying to sleep in their bed with them.

Fearful of not being able to feed her children, Mom got herself a job as a cashier at a supermarket near Madison Heights, Michigan, where my parents bought their first home. My mom was born in Detroit, but she left it when she was just a tyke, after her mom divorced her dad and returned to the family base in Omaha, Nebraska. But after my brother Bill was born, two years after Kevin died, my dad went on a drinking rampage and found himself again jobless. So my mom contacted her father back in Detroit. She had not seen him in twenty years, but he told her to come to the Motor City and he would do what he could.

It was in the Detroit area that my brother Terence and I were born. But with each new birth came added stress on the marriage. My mom did everything she could to make us feel as if everything was normal, but the duct tape around the pole of the artificial tree couldn't hide the fact that Mom had been up all night trying to put the pieces of her sons' Christmas back together after Dad knocked everything over in a drunken rage.

Right before my mom and dad split up—in what was probably a last-ditch effort to pretend things were normal—they were in the process of buying a beautiful new quad-level house in the Eastwood Manor subdivision, located in a better part of Madison Heights, off 13 Mile Road instead of 10½. (In Detroit, the farther you get from 8 Mile, the better.) The orphanage she'd been placed in as a child had scarred Mom deeply, so living in new surroundings was something she set out to do from that point on, and she has lived in nothing but a series of newly constructed homes ever since. When we were picking out colors and finishes at Eastwood Manor, each of us boys was told we could pick out what color carpeting we would have in our bedrooms. (It was plush carpeting, as shag was so over by then.) I can't recall what Terence or I picked, but we all remember when my brother Bill suggested "moss green" for his room.

Mom wasn't having it.

"Sure, Billy. And then we can paint the walls *shithouse brown*," Mom replied to her nine-year-old son, her rocky marriage never chipping away at her sarcastic wit. I couldn't get my parents to spring for the Crayola box of sixty-four colors, but I looked through my friend Andrew's and not once did I come across that shade. My brother ended up picking another color.

But the move to the new house never happened. Finally, in 1972, after four sons and thirteen years of marriage, my mom had had enough. Years of physical and emotional abuse. Years of uncertainty. Years of anxiety. That my mom's mother had committed suicide and was no longer around to say "I told you so" surely weighed into my mom's decision, but it was a culmination of many things. My mom left my dad. I was four.

Dad did not take the news well. He started showing up at my mom's work and harassed her, going so far as to try to tackle her to the ground and take her car keys. He started showing up at my brothers' elementary school to try to talk Billy into leaving with him. At first there was an attempt at a "weekend dad" situation. But my mom did not want our father to come into our house, since it was the place where most of his abuse took place. The judges in the early '70s were convinced my mom was "just being hysterical" when she requested that Dad not be allowed to visit us at our home—as if someone like my dad were going to abruptly stop his abusive ways because he no longer lived there—but my mom's demands were mostly ignored. Efforts to turn my dad into a responsible weekend father were ill-fated from the beginning, but no one could have predicted just how badly.

After a weekend visit at his sketchy apartment in nearby Hazel Park, which was more like a depressing room in a group house of some kind, he piled us into his avocado green Datsun 210 station wagon one Sunday evening and drove head-on into a lamppost directly in front of the local police station—blind drunk. A random woman on the street raced over to comfort my brothers and me as we tumbled out of the backseat, not really sure what had happened. She then reached down and picked Terence up, perhaps thinking he was the youngest as I had quickly grown taller than him, despite being two-and-a-half years younger. But I didn't want a stand-in for my mother anyway. None of us was seriously injured, but the scars were already visible to anyone who was looking.

Once inside the police station, I saw my mom and her new boyfriend (Gary) in the distance, running through the halls as we sat in one of the detectives' offices. Mom immediately bent down and picked me up, hugging and kissing me as she repeatedly asked me if I was OK. I was now.

My horrified mother quickly moved to have Dad's visitation rights revoked, and the judge didn't think she was being quite so hysterical this time around.

Then, less than a year later, Dad wound up disoriented in a Veterans Administration hospital in Allen Park, Michigan. Just forty years old, my father had morphed—seemingly overnight—into a helpless old man (or young child?), suffering from what doctors variously called "organic brain syndrome," "psychosis," and "dementia."

His files would later reveal that doctors perceived him to be "extremely bright" but with "little insight into his situation." The cause? Unknown. His sons, Billy, age eleven; Terence, age eight; and Kenny, age six, were perceived by their schoolteachers as "extremely bright" but with little insight into their father's situation. So all the Walsh men were as bright as they were confused? That was putting it mildly.

The doctors theorized that his brain injury was caused by a blow to the head (not hard to picture, given my dad's big mouth and penchant for picking fights) or alcohol poisoning (also not hard to envision: My dad had always been a beer drinker, but there were unconfirmed rumors of an empty bottle of vodka in his room at the flophouse where he was living after the car accident, and he could have thoughtlessly guzzled it down). Whatever the cause, it erased his short-term memory, so when he was asked to provide his phone number and address, he reverted to his married life—the last life he apparently remembered—and gave them his old information.

Now recently remarried and hoping to shield her three young boys from the additional horrors of what was to come, my mother made the decision to have my father's nephew (whose family was in the nursing-home business) bring Dad back to his hometown of Pottsville, Pennsylvania, to be near his large family. And that was that.

We were all too young to have a say in the matter. We'd seen plenty already—sometimes taking refuge in motels (a Holiday Inn in Hazel Park) or at friends' houses when Dad went off the rails. Mom had to do what she thought was best, and she made the difficult decision that it would be in everyone's best interest not to have him and his unstable life as part of our day-to-day existence. But I don't remember anyone ever explaining what was going on. It was as if one day we had a father, however erratic, and the next day he vanished. No discussion. No visit. No good-bye. Just as had happened with my mother and her father, I did not see my dad for the next twenty years.

Decades later, I would learn that Dad would sometimes call my mother up and say he was "ready to go home," as if nothing had ever happened.

The birth of my (half) sister, Jennifer, in 1974 and our move to Arizona in 1979, when I nearly twelve, were pivotal in forcing me to "move on," although not everyone in the family handled things the same way.

My brother Bill, being the oldest, was closest to our dad, but it was my middle brother, Terence, who took the situation hardest. He resented our stepfather, Gary, enormously and never missed an opportunity to (unfairly) remind him that he felt Gary was an intruder in our lives. Bill was far too close to my dad to accept Gary as the new man in the house, and although I was young enough to be more receptive, I followed my brothers' lead and never even considered calling Gary "Dad."

Although I know my mother did what she thought was right, it still confuses me that she never had any sort of communication with my dad's nephew, to whom she was close enough to reach out when she decided Dad should return to Pennsylvania. Equally confusing, none of the Walsh family ever reached out to us. We never got so much as a birthday card or a note from any of them.

There were no updates of any kind, much less any talk of visiting. While we lived in Detroit and later even farther away in Phoenix, our family made periodic visits to the East Coast to see my mom's extended family in Maryland, so a trip to Pennsylvania would not have been logistically out of the question.

All of this silence became the norm for me, but it also bathed me in intense shame. Stepparents just weren't as commonplace in the mid-'70s, and I was almost always the only kid in class whose mother had a different last name. (Those damn Brady girls couldn't wait to take Mike's name!) It was excruciatingly difficult trying to explain to my peers where my dad was when even I didn't know, myself.

I knew he wasn't remarried or living a normal life somewhere, because we knew he was institutionalized someplace. But the word *dementia* did not become commonplace until decades later, so I would routinely tell people that my dad was a "vegetable." While I would learn much, much later that this was quite far from the truth, it was the closest term I could think of that fit, and it usually shut people up and prevented follow-up questions.

This situation was not acceptable to Terence. Unbeknownst to any of us, he began secretly corresponding with one of our dad's nephews, but Terence didn't tell Bill or me until well after our grandmother had passed away and Uncle Kenny had died of cancer the year after his mother's death. Uncle Kenny had been in his forties.

When my brother finally let these two big news items slip, he confessed that he was afraid my mom would feel betrayed if she knew he had been in touch with the Walshes, a sad admission. My mom swore that couldn't have been further from the truth. While I didn't necessarily agree with Terence's thinking, I also remember feeling a desire to protect my mom, who had taken her share of beatings from this man. How would it make her feel if we pined for him?

But by the early 1990s, both of my brothers, who had relocated to the East Coast just before I did, had gone to see Dad at the VA hospital in Lebanon, Pennsylvania, where he had been living since 1974. The code of silence continued, however. They were horrified by what they saw; there seemed to be no separation between residents who were disabled and those who were deranged. So they kept the visit to themselves. By the time I got to Washington in early 1993, though, the laws had changed, and veterans who had not been injured during active duty were no longer welcome to live in VA facilities, so our dad's nephew had arranged for Dad to move into a "nicer" nursing home nearby, *nicer* being a relative term in these living arrangements.

I had just started a job at the National Gallery of Art in the summer of 1993 when my brothers arranged to take me to see Dad, exactly twenty years since the last time I had laid eyes on him. The anxiety leading up to that trip was so unbearable I had to leave work early several days that week, a move that did not ingratiate me with my new boss.

My childhood memories of my father had long been a haze of two extremes. There was the horrifying reality of being thrown through a paneled wall as a four-year-old boy while trying to pull him off my mother during one of his drunken tirades. I donned my brother Bill's hockey gear in a failed attempt to intimidate him. There were the visits to the sketchy places he was living right after he and my mom separated: a room at the dingy John R Motel, where we watched the coverage after George Wallace was shot during the 1972 Democratic primary race (we knew who Wallace was because the famed segregationist was the preferred candidate of our hillbilly neighbors, the Blys, who had signs in their windows and yard) and the group house Dad was living in when his brain injury occurred, filled with what we all remember as being "big, scary men." But I also remembered joyous times, like when Dad bought me a plastic pumpkin on a stick for Halloween. Or Dad making me giggle uncontrollably while chasing me up the stairs at Notre Dame stadium, a remembrance that I likely constructed from whole cloth based on an old photograph that I allowed my imagination to bring to life.

Many years had passed, for sure, but to suddenly walk into a room and see the "big, strong man" I remembered as a child being spoon-fed blenderized turkey and drinking out of a sippy cup was like a blow to my own head.

The first time the nurses took me to see him, they took the formal step of "introducing" me to him. He looked me right in the eye and said, "I have a son named Kenny."

It still stings to think about it today.

The visits over the next twelve years would never get any easier. If anything, they seemed to become increasingly painful, as the foolish notion that he might "get better" faded completely.

Instead, I became increasingly angry. Why had this happened to him? He had his problems, but he also had so much to live for—like three boys who needed their father. The room, the smell, the whole place. It was hard to imagine your father living in a situation like that for over thirty years, and each return was another reminder of his pathetic existence. He would continually forget who you were if he remembered at any point at all. He would repeat the same question over and over and over. He would tell the same "joke" over and over and over. Sometimes he would get agitated and make inappropriate comments. Frequently, he would make lurid remarks about having sex with my mom that would make me want to punch him. Apparently the expression "Wham, bam, thank you, ma'am" had been particularly funny the year his brain stopped acquiring new information.

But every so often I'd catch a glimpse of the Dad I (sort of) remembered. He could talk about things from twenty years ago with precise detail, so if you could keep him from getting into one of his loops, it could often make for a heartwarming experience, for at least a few minutes. Because he worked for General Motors, cars was also a good subject.

"What kind of car did you have in 1968, Dad?" my brother Bill would ask him.

Although my dad worked in Detroit during its automotive heyday, he was a trailblazer in buying Japanese cars that got great gas mileage. (Detroit might have survived if only auto executives had listened to my dad and started making better cars sooner.)

Sometimes I tried to go deeper. Once I even asked about Kevin. Dad couldn't remember who was in the room from one minute to the next, but the second I asked him about his firstborn, a change came over his entire body, and he winced as if it were March 1960 all over again, finding his little boy dead in his crib.

What was fascinating was that every once in a while, the "current" version of him would hint at his old smart-ass self—

like when he would tease the other residents and the nurses, or the way he was always annoyed by his latest "jackass roommate" and wanting to punch someone. (I certainly know where I get my lack of tolerance for people from, although my mom wasn't a particular help in that department, either!)

But no sooner would the old Dad appear than he would slip away, and my heart would break all over again. Another couple of years would go by before I could work up the emotional fortitude to come back.

I just couldn't stop thinking about the person my aunt Clara would talk about, who was so smart, so funny, and so charming I almost felt she secretly wished she had married Dad instead of his older brother Joe. ("And he was such a great speller!") While my mother may have chosen not to try to keep Dad "alive" when we were little—no visits, no regular phone calls with his caretakers—she was always open to talking about him, rarely portraying him in anything but a favorable light.

"Your father was a good man," she always says. "He just couldn't handle his drinking."

Mom traces his troubles back to his childhood, when his father died after falling off a roof he was working on. Dad, who was just thirteen, and his seven siblings went from being local royalty to objects of pity overnight. (My grandmother Stella never remarried, but she did have extended family to help her out.)

Mom also traces Dad's downfall to his time in the Korean War. Although he and his twin were so charismatic they were selected to pose in photos with the actress Betty Hutton, fresh off her Golden Globe nomination for *Annie Get Your Gun*, when she came through Korea on a USO tour, Kenny and Dad also found themselves throwing grenades at the enemy and guarding prisoners of war. And as traumatic as that was, their experience in the military had far more scarring consequences. When my dad and Uncle Kenny enlisted at age eighteen, their nephew Billy Lindes—who was really more like a cousin since he was my dad's oldest sister's son—lied about his age so he could tag along. (He was sixteen.) But when Dad and Uncle Kenny got their orders to go straight to Korea, they contacted their local congressman to come clean about Billy Lindes's age, hoping to ensure he was not sent into combat. My dad was relieved when the congressman pulled some strings and Billy was sent to Okinawa instead of the front lines. But in the confusion of it all, Billy didn't get the required immunizations and wound up dying of encephalitis. The family was devastated—and my mom believes Dad never forgave himself, a burden that followed him as he drank himself into oblivion.

Strangely, near the end of Dad's life, he was far more lucid than he had been during the first decade I had become reacquainted with him. Even his doctor noticed the change, which was certainly not normal for dementia patients. Just before my dad died, Michael and I drove down to see him one weekend. It was the first time I had visited without one of my brothers. For reasons that make perfect sense to me, Dad never had a hard time remembering Terence, who looks very much like Dad's late twin, Kenny, the person to whom Dad was closest. I was eager to see if he would recognize me—his youngest boy—if I was by myself. Michael and I pulled up at Resthaven in our rented PT Cruiser that afternoon, and I had my guy wait in the hallway so I would have Dad's undivided attention—and could put him to the test.

I nervously turned the corner of his floor, my heart racing at 150 beats per minute, and entered the room. His face lit up like an Irishman at the Guinness Factory, as he screamed out "Hey!" in recognition. He may have even started to call me Terence, but I was so happy he "knew" me as his son that I honestly don't even recall.

I crawled into bed with him (he was frail from the radiation treatment he'd been receiving for lung cancer) and stroked his head as we talked and talked for a long time. I was so wrapped up in the only father-son moment we'd ever shared that I completely forgot I'd brought company. Suddenly Dad looked up over my shoulder toward the doorway and saw Michael—who could easily pass for one of Dad's strapping blue-eyed brothers in their youth. Dad got quiet, then sheepishly whispered in my ear, "Is he related to *us*?" Somehow, these were without question the five sweetest words I've ever heard.

escape *from* new york?

It was hot and sunny, and the Puerto Rican Day parade was in full swing that June afternoon when my cat, Troy, and I pulled up to our new Chelsea abode, with a moving van in hot pursuit.

It had been only a matter of weeks since I had put in a request for a job transfer to my company's just-opened New York bureau. But in reality, the move had been a quarter-of-a-century in the making. So I was relieved as much as I was happy, finally putting an end to a lifetime of feeling as if I was missing out on something.

As broke college students, my friend Greg and I used to drive to desolate downtown Phoenix, where five buildings pretended to be a skyline, to make believe we were living the city life. We even took the bus once, abandoning our car in a suburban Jack-in-the-Box parking lot, just to experience "mass transit." There was just one restaurant that was open twenty-four hours—a Mexican joint called the Matador, on East Adams Street—so we'd go there and buy coffee, then fill up on free chips and salsa and pretend we were cool. Now I really was living in Manhattan, and there was no need to pretend.

I stayed up until everything was unpacked and in its new home that first night, then slept soundly knowing that no matter what happened next, it would be all right. If I didn't already secretly fancy myself as Mary Richards moving into her new place after a breakup—we were both thirty-one and newsroom gals—my sister cemented the idea by mailing me a giant wooden letter *K* that Christmas. Now it was up to me to provide the "Etc."

But no sooner did I get to New York than I was informed that the only thing "real" New Yorkers want to do in the summer is get the hell out of New York. Confused by the new rules and regulations, I turned to my friend Ken, who had also moved to New York from Washington earlier that spring.

Ken had transferred too, so having our same jobs and same best friends from Washington in New York was an odd feeling for both of us. We found ourselves sitting around bars and coffee joints in Chelsea complaining about our love lives and jobs, instead of sitting around bars and coffee joints in Dupont Circle complaining about our love lives and jobs. That I instantly felt at home made sense, though. The backdrop finally matched my story line. It was exactly how I imagined transgender people feel when they finally transition into the sex they were supposed to be, minus the genital reconstruction and increased risk of unemployment, homelessness, and murder.

It was too late for Ken and me to get in on a summer share—which we were informed was the thing gay New Yorkers do—so we took an experimental day trip to Fire Island for a glimpse into our future. I wanted to love it, but a mere afternoon there and I looked like Rip Van Winkle just waking up in Tanzania without a mosquito net. I've read the little pests favor certain people's blood over others, and I don't need scientific research to know it's true. I've never been to a cookout, beach, or outdoor concert without ending up covered in bites—and reeking of Deep Woods Off. Fire Island was no exception

Undeterred, Ken and I instead began to make regular summer jaunts to Europe—*city* jaunts, to London and Paris, mostly—which were made more cost-effective by Ken's status as a pilot and his designation of me as his proxy wife.

After going to London a few times in a row, we decided to mix it up one year and flew into London with plans to go on to Ireland, for an honest-to-God "get out of the city" holiday. It was my birthday the day we traveled, so Ken arranged for us to be in business class as a surprise—my first time flying without using my knee caps as a chin rest. The plan was to arrive in London that night, go to the hotel and freshen up, and then hit the bars to celebrate. We would fly to Ireland a day or two later.

Things quickly turned sour when we went to check in and I realized I'd left my carry-on bag—which had all of my most important belongings, including my passport and our travel itineraries—in the back of the black cab. At first, we weren't too panicked. The hotel staff seemed confident that we'd be able to get my stuff back from the "Lost Property Office." With a name so quaint, I thought, how could they not be honest? Confident of an imminent happy ending to the great missing-bag caper, I managed to put the problem out of my mind long enough to go out and celebrate my birthday.

That night at the Pink Pounder was a memorable one—well, as memorable as a night at pub called the Pink Pounder can be. Cute guys everywhere. Great music all night (play Neneh Cherry's "Buffalo Stance" once and you can pretty much do anything after that). We must have met a couple dozen men, including a hot guy in overalls named David whom I went home with. (And I thought Britain didn't have gyms.)

The next morning wasn't so memorable, though. At least not the kind of memorable you want to hold on to. I don't know how much alcohol they put in the beer over there—British people always sound as if they're slurring their words to me, so I figure it's more—but I became violently ill afterward. My real-life Michelangelo kindly told me I could stay in bed until I felt better, but he had to go to work. When I finally got up, it was only to stumble into the bathroom so I could vomit some more. It was on my way back to the bedroom that I met David's "flatmate," who seemed nice enough until I realized he was wearing nothing but blue bikini underwear and just happened to be watching a porno video at 8 a.m. While his shirtless state accentuated his nonthreatening curved British shoulders and bitch tits, I still sensed I was in for trouble. Before I could even come to terms with what I was seeing, he exposed himself—and he wasn't doing it emotionally. I was in a bad way, but even I recognized that this took the term *sloppy seconds* to a whole new level: masturbating in front of your roommate's discarded trick who's vomiting all over the house the morning after? More like *sickly seconds.* I nearly started crying.

After getting dressed and pulling myself together, I made a quick exit. Somehow, I managed to meet up with Ken at a restaurant—with no cell phones and being in a foreign country, neither of us today is quite sure how this happened—where I was so hungover and so upset about my lost belongings that I finally did burst into tears right there at the table. Ken was reeling at the details of what had just happened with the flatmate, and has spent the past decade insisting that the real reason I got so distraught is that I actually jerked the guy off as the tears flowed. (I maintain my innocence.)

We were supposed to be leaving for the Emerald Isle in the morning, but we ended up waiting around London through the weekend and into the next week—all time that was meant to be spent in the Irish countryside—under the belief that British taxi drivers were honest, yet my stuff never turned up.

Much to my surprise, I became extremely emotional when I called the American Embassy to see what I had to do about getting a replacement passport. Something about being outside of the United States without proper documentation got to me, so when someone with an American accent answered the phone, I lost it again. Luckily, I still had my souvenir American Airlines business-class blankie, which would prove to be most useful while lying on the floor crying in the fetal position.

The following day we finally gave up on my lost bag and headed to the U.S. Embassy first thing in the morning. It turns out this happens a lot, so we hung out on the steps with two dozen other careless Americans. Getting the passport took all of ten minutes. This was pre-9/11, so all I had to do was have Ken "vouch" that I was an American, and they issued a new one on the spot. Later in the day, we finally made it to Ireland for an abbreviated stay. We hoped it would help us forget the unfortunate string of events that had led to this point—the bikini-underwear incident first and foremost.

A quick stay in Dublin was fun, although it might have been even better if our hotel, the Inn on the Liffey, hadn't turned out to double as the saddest bathhouse in Western Europe. "The Troubles" paled in comparison to what I saw inside that place.

Having lost all of our paperwork and travel itineraries, I placed a long-distance phone call to a colleague back in New York and talked him through logging onto my work e-mail and finding all of the information we needed to proceed. (This was a much bigger feat in the year 2000 than it is today.)

We then drove west toward Galway, the part of Ireland from which I believed my great-grandfather emigrated to the United States. Unlike Dublin, Galway is a mostly rural area—and this was meant to be a "relaxing, away-from-the-city" vacation—but as the city views gave way to empty fields, I could feel my heart begin to race.

Somehow, we managed to find the nondescript subdivision where it turned out the bed-and-breakfast I had booked on the Internet was located.

Although Ken was busy driving, he noticed something was horribly wrong with me. It had been only ten years since I left typically American suburban life, but after a decade in West Hollywood, Washington, and now Manhattan, I was a changed person. (Or had I always been this way? I spent my formative years in Arizona, yet never visited the Grand Canyon. I just couldn't see sitting in a smoke- and bicker-filled station wagon when I could have the house to myself.) Suddenly, the prospect of staying in a stranger's quiet house—in the middle of nowhere—became too overwhelming for my city self.

Before Ken could decide what course of action to take, we noticed a sweet, ruddy-cheeked woman in a flower-print housedress standing in the driveway, waving as she noticed the familiar sight of an unfamiliar car.

"Turn around," I gasped, a full-blown panic attack setting in. "Turn around *right now*!"

Ken had never seen me like this, but he knew me well enough to know I was not kidding around. Already struggling to stay on the wrong side of the road, Ken then made an abrupt U-turn in the cul-de-sac, nearly sideswiping the horrified innkeeper as dust blew in her face, and floored it.

"Are you OK, Kenneth?" Ken asked, as the bed-and-breakfast faded into the distance.

"I think so," I said. "We just need to find the city."

As I began to calm down, my polite side was feeling horribly guilty about the way we treated this poor woman. Still, I ultimately couldn't help but fault her for living in the middle of nowhere.

After our bed-and-breakfast drive-by, we pulled out the map and headed to Galway City. We had no idea what was there, but at least it had the word *city* in it. It wasn't far, so we quickly found a charming hotel in the heart of the little downtown area with a twenty-four-hour restaurant and wash 'n' fold laundry service. The city wasn't much to speak of—a few restaurants, a few clothing shops, and a few pubs—but at least there was something.

After getting situated in our room and procuring some tips from the concierge, Ken and I decided to check out the nightlife.

While scanning Galway's three blocks of action, we discovered there was even a gay bar—a sure sign of city life—and I felt enormous relief when we got inside, where the music was pumping and we were far away from the great outdoors. It helped that all five of the guys inside were really friendly, too.

I read an article in the *New York Times* a few years later about a group of urban Hurricane Katrina survivors who were temporarily relocated to the Baptist Vista Encampment, a summer retreat in the Ozark Mountains in northwestern Arkansas. The evacuees, accustomed to city life in New Orleans, were not prepared for the change of scenery.

The *Times* wrote:

"All these trees," a woman named Betty sobbed, as her husband, Ray, and her two sisters tried to comfort her. "It seems like hell." Her husband, a landscaper in New Orleans, wiped away a tear as well. "It's scary," he said.

How I could empathize with Betty and Ray's arbor day of reckoning. And that was when I realized I wasn't alone: Despite what the New Yorker manual might tell you, some of us just don't have the "get out of the city" gene. While most urbanites find escapes to be relaxing, the idea of being someplace where you can't go to the corner store twenty-four hours a day and where you don't run a greater-than-average chance of being murdered triggers panic attacks in me. I suspect I got through my suburban childhood only because I never really knew when my mom might snap.

All these years later, I now have friends with homes in the Hamptons who kindly invite us out for the weekend every summer. But I'm secretly grateful that Michael has to work some weekends so we "just can't."

The truth is, it took me thirty-one exhausting years to finally get *in* the city. So why would I ever want to get out?

the one-armed love bandit

I was standing in the middle of a thousand shirtless men at New York's annual Chelsea Pier Dance when it hit me. It was Gay Pride weekend, yet looking around I never felt more ashamed. I was tired of not having one of *those* bodies. You know what I'm talking about: smooth, defined chest, bulging biceps, tiny waist—and, of course, ripped abs.

At 6 feet, 150 pounds, I somehow managed to avoid all these attributes. My arms were sticks. My puny pecs could barely excite a NAMBLA member. And God forbid you needed a shoulder to cry on. Worse yet, even though I would be considered malnourished on most U.S. government height/weight charts, I still was beginning to have a midlife spare tire and love handles—well, at least by gay standards. People always say advertising and the media put so much pressure on women to look a certain way, but being a gay man in New York City—birthplace of the "Chelsea boy"—is surely no easier. In fact, I'd venture to say Chelsea was the birthplace of "mean girls."

A friend of mine had just read the latest fitness book and had suddenly transformed himself into one of those guys who takes off his shirt at the club and everyone goes crazy. I was determined to do the same.

I quickly became obsessed. Going to the gym seven days a week—frequently twice a day—became the norm. I ate nothing but canned tuna, chicken breasts, and protein shakes. Within three months I, too, had transformed my body. Although I hadn't really gained much muscle, I was very defined and had attained something many find hardest of all: perfect washboard abs.

The attention was instant and very gratifying. First, a friend of mine snapped a roll of film of me for my new-and-improved AOL profile. Guys who had never noticed me before were suddenly begging to hook up. The locker room at my gym—once a place where I couldn't get arrested—had suddenly become a veritable singles bar. At parties, my friends would insist that I lift my shirt up to show off "the six-pack." All of this gave me a lot of confidence, and it wasn't too long before I started to go out with a newfound vengeance.

It was a Sunday night at local bar when I saw this really handsome thirtysomething former-frat-boy type across the room. I glanced over at him and his not-nearly-as-attractive friend a couple of times, and it wasn't long before they came over to say hi. At first the friend did most of the talking, but I kept smiling at the cute one, and in one of those rare, perfect gay-bar moments, I was actually getting the guy I wanted instead of talking to someone I wasn't interested in for nine hours.

His name was Mark. Tall, athletic, and very good-looking, he told me he was a ski instructor, with some kind of former-investment-banker thing going on. I was ready for a ride down the slopes.

Soon, the bar's requisite drag show began, and my new friend and I moved to the back to watch it together. We drank and laughed at the show, and he'd hug me from behind, kissing my neck periodically. We later moved over by the pinball machine and started making out for a good twenty minutes before we began negotiating moving this party somewhere else. He was in town preparing to move back from the Left Coast and I lived down the street, so the deal to go back to my place was virtually sealed until he suddenly turned serious.

"I just want to make sure you're clear about something," he said. Clear about *something*? I knew this wasn't going to be good. Expecting him to reveal that perhaps he had a boyfriend or was HIV-positive, I played it cool and calmly said, "Sure, what's that?"

Motioning his head toward his left arm slightly, he looked back at me straight in the eyes and said, "I just want to make sure you're aware of *this*."

"Huh?" I thought to my stunned self.

"This," it seemed, was his prosthetic arm, which suddenly couldn't be missed from atop the Empire State Building.

Granted, the bar was packed, and once we met we were never more than an inch away from each other. And sure, I was a little drunk. But even I was having a hard time explaining to myself how I had missed that one. Immediately sensing the gravity of the moment, my mind raced for an answer. If I suddenly had to get up early in the morning (or needed to "wash my hair"!) then surely he would know I was a *limbist*. I was so into him up until this moment, there could be no other explanation. If I lied and said that of course I noticed, I'd be in bed with an amputee in about ten minutes.

Although it felt like I must have stood there frozen for at least an hour (I was mostly wondering if this scene was being captured on video surveillance and how hard it would be for me to buy a copy), I actually managed a quick and casual "Yeah, of course I am." Mark looked pleased, grabbed my hand (with his real arm), and out the door we went.

The walk home was a blur, but back at my place we kissed a little more on the sofa before Mark excused himself to go the bathroom to "get ready." A couple minutes later out he came, in nothing but a pair of white boxer shorts. Just as I'd imagined, he had a "gym body": strong and muscular and *perfect* but for the fact that his left arm—every last inch of it—was gone. I, too, excused myself to get ready and my cat, Troy, followed me into the bathroom. My heart was racing. I felt ashamed of myself for being frightened, but deep down I truly was. I sat down on the toilet to collect my thoughts for a moment when I noticed through the clear shower curtain that Mark had left his "arm" in my shower stall. Troy took one look at it, jumped back three feet, and began to hiss. His tail tripled in size, and the hair stood up on his back as I thought to myself, "I know, I know," and stumbled for the medicine cabinet to find the Viagra my friend had given me "for fun." I started to panic. How am I going to get through this? I had only experimented with the boner pills once before, but I was told that the 100 mg tablets should be broken in half or even fourths. I swallowed one whole.

Back in my bedroom we fooled around a little, but pharmaceutical aid or not, I wasn't really up for much. When we had reached a plausible stopping point, the thing that did pop up on my bed was the journalist in me. I needed to know *everything*. Mark was very sweet as he told me about the tumor that cost him his arm and about some of the daily challenges he faces as a result of it. After about an hour of cross-examination he left.

For days afterward I was pretty shaken. I felt ashamed of myself for so many reasons that I'm embarrassed to even admit. I couldn't sleep at night or concentrate at the office during the day. Eventually I pulled a friend at work aside and confided what had happened. She was sympathetic and tried to tell me how admirable it was that I'd gone through with the hookup. But somehow this just made me feel worse.

Mark didn't deserve, much less *need*, to have me patronize him, yet all I could think was how brave he was to walk out of that bathroom naked and make himself so vulnerable in front of a complete stranger. I thought about all the times I'd been so ashamed of my body in the locker room and how shallow I'd been for being so consumed with my appearance.

Mark called me once or twice in the months that followed. He was living in New York now and wondered if I'd like to get together again. By then I was seeing Michael pretty seriously, so I took a pass on the offer. I also decided to take a pass on working out twice a day, drinking Myoplex shakes in lieu of eating real food, and constantly beating myself up for not having the perfect body. Although becoming intensely focused on fitness had garnered me attention I deeply craved, it had also stopped me from doing virtually everything else I enjoyed. I was finally able to admit to myself that the real reason my abs were popping out of stomach was because I was down to a mere 138 pounds, which at 6 feet also left my face looking gaunt and tired. (I might have figured something was amiss when I began having to special-order size 28/34 chinos from the Gap, and they were still falling off my waist.) Perhaps moderation really was the best way to go.

My tryst with the one-armed love bandit may not have been steamiest night of my life, but the lasting sense of perspective it's given me has been far more life-changing than even the best set of washboard abs could ever be.

bud, bath and beyond

I'd been living in my Manhattan apartment for about a decade when I noticed something odd as I was heading into the shower one afternoon. My toothbrush was in the wrong hole in my shower caddy. I'm hardly Felix Unger; it's just that putting your toothbrush back in its proper place is, as my friend Jay put it, like turning off the oven: You don't really remember doing it, but you know you do.

I also used to keep one in the built-in toothbrush holder next to the bathroom sink, but my cat, Larry, has adopted it as his own, gnawing on it after every feeding and between-meal snack.

Perplexed but still believing there must be a logical explanation, I moved my toothbrush to its proper spot—the right-front hole of the shower caddy—then went about my business. When I spoke to Michael later that afternoon, I figured he would simply tell me that he had moved it for some reason or other, maybe while getting out his visitor razor or something—we've been together for more than a decade but don't want to rush into living together—and that would the end of it.

"Why would I move your toothbrush?" he snapped, immediately annoyed, as if he'd been falsely accused of a home-invasion rape-murder combo. As I tried to explain that he was merely a person of interest, I added, trying hard to sound casual, "Well, are you sure you didn't accidentally knock it out and then put it back in the wrong hole?" I knew it was virtually impossible to "knock" my toothbrush from its place, but I hoped the answer would be yes.

"No, I didn't touch it," he growled. Then he refused to speak to me for the remainder of the day.

I went to work in the newsroom that evening—I was doing 6 p.m. to 1 a.m. at the time, admittedly the preferred shift of conspiracy theorists—and spent the next twenty-four hours not sure what to think. Part of me was trying to convince myself that I wasn't crazy—the toothbrush had moved, of this I was certain—while the other part was terrified at the prospect that it had. (How would this even be possible?) I wasn't sure which was worse.

The following afternoon, I got up at my usual time and began my daily routine. Having just woken up, I'd momentarily let the Mystery of the Misplaced Toothbrush slip from my mind, but as I entered the bathroom—which is only slightly bigger than an airplane lavatory—I peeked through my clear shower curtain to find that my toothbrush had once again moved ... into the back right corner of the caddy. I have never been so scared in my life. Had someone broken into my apartment while I was sleeping? Was that someone in the apartment right now? I felt like Julia Roberts in *Sleeping with the Enemy,* only with considerably smaller teeth. My entire home is the size of a master bathroom in exurbia, yet suddenly it felt like a giant not-so-funhouse with a million places to hide. After a quick check of the closet and behind the doors, I frantically called Michael. I don't really remember what happened next, although I'm told I began screaming at him, demanding to know if he had moved it this time just to fuck with me.

"I swear, Kenny. I didn't touch your toothbrush," he said, "I have no idea what's going on." While he didn't respond kindly to my initial "accusation," he could tell I was truly frightened this time and cut me some slack as I began to unhinge.

When I calmed down for a minute, I made a quick mental list of who had keys to my apartment. Other than a friend who doesn't live anywhere near New York, the list was short:

Normando, my directly-below-me downstairs neighbor, buddy, and cat sitter; and Tony, my super, to whom I begrudgingly gave a key years ago after a flood upstairs left my shower ceiling nearly caved in. I say "begrudgingly" because the last super who had a key to my apartment, Mr. Whorley—the guy in charge of my first apartment in Washington, D.C., whom I'd only spoken to once or twice after signing my lease—let himself into my sixth-floor efficiency to decorate it with balloons and confetti for my twenty-six birthday, an efficient way to creep me into prematurely moving out.

I called Tony the super and asked if he or anyone else from the management company had been in my place for any reason. He said no. He was using a motorized wheelchair at that point and could not climb stairs anymore, rendering him a super in title only, but I figured I had to ask. When I told him why I was inquiring, he began to giggle. "I left the remote control in the kitchen, Kennett" (he can't make the *th* sound, a common trait among Hispanics that never fails to endear me to them), "and I spent a half an hour looking for it in the living room!" he explained. I said that I understood what he was talking about but that this was not one of those just-being-forgetful cases, but he just laughed.

With Tony ruled out as a suspect, I began to get even more anxious, my hands shaking and my mind racing. If it was not someone with a legal right to be there, then who could be entering my apartment—and more disturbing, why? What were they doing with my toothbrush—which, of course, I was no longer using but was leaving in the caddy as a decoy. And what other personal items might they be "using" that I wasn't aware of? With no time to call a locksmith, I put up a handwritten sign on the bathroom mirror that read "YOU ARE BEING WATCHED," although that seemed to be directed as much at me as it was at any intruders stopping by to freshen up. Although I was sick at the thought of leaving my apartment unguarded, I had to get to work. Once there, I explained to a few of my colleagues the mini-horror flick I'd been living. My pal Jesse was immediately sympathetic and didn't seem to question my story, but he was in the definite minority.

Our supervisor, Lynn, rolled her eyes and proceeded to give me a long lecture about logic and absurdity. "No one would break into your apartment just to move your toothbrush," she concluded. "People do things that they forget all the time. You're being ridiculous."

As word of the Great Toothbrush Caper traveled around the newsroom, I was greeted with one skeptical face after another. (And you people call yourself journalists? I thought.) If they weren't accusing me of being overly dramatic, they were humoring me by suggesting that I set up a "nanny cam" in my bathroom. (Not a bad idea, I figured.)

Jesse, the office realist, asked me a few questions, and when he heard that the only other person with a key was my neighbor/cat sitter, he suggested calling Normando and casually asking him if he'd seen anyone who looked suspicious in our building. That way, Jesse reasoned, even though I had no basis to suspect my buddy, I could eliminate him as a suspect without coming off as accusatory. Plus, if anyone would have seen something, it's Normando. Our five-story building is far from glamorous, a walk-up with no doorman and the occasional used cotton swab left on the stairs for weeks on end. (Tony the super is either blind, doesn't care, or can no longer bend over to pick them up.) But Normando, a handsome-in-his day, gay Puerto Rican man who didn't appear to be old enough to retire (early sixties, perhaps) but didn't seem to have a job, was like our de facto security guard. Each day he would stand on our stoop, leaning against the railing, keeping an eye on the comings and goings of our Chelsea building. He was the ideal possible witness.

As the night turned to morning, and with the laughter of all of those naysayers echoing in my head, I managed to convince myself that the toothbrush hadn't actually moved again; I'd just forgotten to move it to its proper home when I originally noticed it had been moved, I told myself. Deep down, I knew this wasn't true. But out of self-preservation I just had to move on, and the thought of calling my neighbor—who had become a dear friend over the years, always looking after my cat and apartment no matter how long I was away—just seemed too absurd, even for me.

A month went by, and my toothbrush stayed in its proper place. I'd pretty much convinced myself that the whole incident had just been "one of those bizarre things" when I headed into the shower one afternoon before work and there it was—back-right hole. This time, the anxiety and horror increased exponentially. I was frozen, the way you are when you find a dead palmetto bug on the floor. You know it can't do anything to you, but it's not really a "palmetto," it's a gigantic cockroach. And the sense of fear and violation is so strong that you believe there is no way you can ever feel safe in your own home again.

At work, I told a whole new group of people—surely this was a front-page story, or at least worth a full page in the Metro section—and again was met with a mixed response, although the terror in my voice had more people believing this time. I happened to have left Normando a message to arrange for him to cat-sit while Michael and I spent a week in Rome. So when he called me back that evening, I decided to follow Jesse's advice from a month earlier, but only after I'd gotten the cat-sitting arrangements finalized.

"So let me ask you something," I delicately said, as if I were going to ask how his week was going. "Have you seen or heard anyone going into my apartment lately?"

"Well, I hear the door, but I just assume it's you," Normando said. "Why?

"There have been a few things moved around in my place, and it seems like someone has been in there," I said. "I was thinking it must be the super, but he denies that he's been over at all."

"Was anything stolen?" Normando asked, sounding concerned.

"No, nothing like that," I explained. "It's just really weird."

"Well," he said, startling me with a pause that is reserved for doctors who are about to tell you the results came back positive—the tumor's malignant. "I have often *fantasized* about coming upstairs to use your shower." The hair stood up on the back of my neck. "You know how awful mine is, switching from freezing cold to scalding hot. But I've never actually done it," he added with a chuckle.

My jaw dropped. This was not the figure-of-speech kind of jaw drop, but the way a sitcom character's does when he discovers that the money he'd found stashed behind the plant and blew at the racetrack was actually for the rent.

No, I did not know "how awful" his shower was—I'd somehow neglected to let myself into his apartment to lather up—but I did know that "fantasies" and middle-aged gay men with a lot of time on their hands were two things you didn't want to think about when learning someone had been surreptitiously hanging out in your apartment.

I said nothing, too stunned to speak and too afraid of what either of us might say next.

"My mother showered at your place when she was in town," he then threw out. "Didn't I tell you about that?"

His *mother*?

Trying to curb my horror, I managed to produce these four words: "Um, no. She did?"

"Yeah. I just couldn't subject her to my shower," he explained. "But that was a few years ago."

Was this Normando's way out of admitting that *he* was making himself at home in my apartment? That it was doing double duty as the New York City franchise of the Bates Motel?

Then, just as my terror was beginning to make room for the slightest hint of relief that came from knowing it wasn't some stranger off the street breaking into my apartment but more of a wacky absent-minded uncle—who, yes, had invited himself over when I wasn't home so he could masturbate with my toothbrush—Normando said one more thing that somehow managed to make the whole thing even worse.

"Well, this is really strange, Kenneth. It's almost like you've been *raped.*"

I had my locks changed later that day.

kenneth in the (212)

The first time I heard the term *Web log*—or *blog* for short—I was editing stories for the "Circuits" section of the *New York Times.* I had recently been hired as a nonpermanent full-time editor (a "casual") when the paper decided to beef up its staff in preparation for the invasion of Iraq, but because I'd been recruited by the *Times* newswire, I was editing stories from all sections of the paper. Shortly thereafter, I had done a Web search about a reality show I had seen—some sort of "hunt for the next male model" type of thing on Bravo—and stumbled upon a site called Towleroad, which I would learn was one of the most popular gay blogs around. I loved the way its author, Andy Towle, was free to write about whatever topic interested him—politics, television, astronomy, men—and the way his readers could leave feedback with their comments.

About two years later, I came home from an incredible match at the U.S. Open between Tommy Haas and Robby Ginepri—one of those late-night battles where everybody moves down from the cheap seats after two-thirds of the stadium clears out—and I wanted to share the experience with everyone I knew. A group e-mail just didn't seem to be enough, so I decided to create a blog. Even as I was setting the whole thing up—picking the name Kenneth in the (212), a nod to Dennis Hensley's *Misadventures in the (213),* a book I had always loved—I was assuming it would be a one-off post, a blog destined to fade into oblivion as most do.

But one "must-share" thought led to another—this was pre-Facebook, pre-Twitter—and before I knew it, I was blogging daily. Concert reviews, movie reviews, book reviews, thoughts on politics, pictures of hot guys, things going on in my personal life, events from my childhood. Everything went. After years of editing other people's words but secretly wishing to express my own, I quickly realized blogging was the perfect outlet for me. I had always thought of myself as a writer, but had never quite found a forum in which I was entirely comfortable. Newspaper reporters were assigned stories—frequently things they did not want to write about—and it's the same with copywriters and technical writers. With blogging, there were no deadlines, no limitations, and, above all, I had total control. It was the complete opposite of every other writing job I had ever tried.

After seeing my blog's readership grow from a handful of charitable friends and family members to hundreds, then thousands—in large part due to an entry I did pointing out the similarities between Valerie Cherish (Lisa Kudrow's brilliant character from her canceled-too-soon HBO show, *The Comeback)* and Madonna (herself on the comeback trail with *Confessions on a Dance Floor* after her disastrous *American Life* album)—I realized people were really responding. A link on the popular LGBT site Queerty was followed by my blog appearing on Towleroad for the first time (a huge moment in any gay blogger's career), Gawker, Romenesko, *New York* magazine's Daily Intel, Perez Hilton, VH1's *Best Week Ever,* and a lead item on the *New York Post*'s infamous Page Six. And in a classic case of "imitation is the sincerest form of flattery," *Entertainment Weekly*—which I lived for in the '90s—twice blatantly ripped off posts from my site. Later, I got invited to blog for the Huffington Post, which pays less than Kenny's Kid Kare did in the early '80s but is great exposure. I wasn't exactly Woodward and Bernstein—or even Michael Musto—but I had finally figured out a way to pursue one of my passions, and I was loving what I was doing for the first time in my life.

Soon, I was being invited to cover all sorts of events around town—plays, book parties, fashion shows, Broadway plays, you name it. The popular sports blog Deadspin referred to Kenneth in the (212) as one of the "leading gay blogs" when referencing a post I wrote about facial hair on football players, and before I knew it, the *Los Angeles Daily News,* the *Los Angeles Times,* and others were calling for my take on LGBT culture and events. Andy Towle even invited me to fill in for him while he was on vacation.

Despite what you may have heard, very few people get rich writing a blog, and only a handful can even eke out a living off the advertising revenue. I was not one of the lucky few. But what I was lacking in blog income I was making up for in opportunities. I was asked to contribute an essay to a book benefiting various animal charities, and then I had my first personal essay published in a popular magazine for gay men. A second soon followed. Later, Susan Olsen—better known as Cindy Brady—asked to include a blog post I had written about the fake Jan who appeared on *The Brady Bunch Variety Hour* in a book she was writing about the show.

Adding to the excitement was that the *New York Times* had finally made an honest man of me, hiring me as a staff editor after three years as a full-time part-timer. Suddenly I had accomplished my childhood dream of working for the Gray Lady. I had never been happier.

All the while, my mom was in a panic about my Internet presence. Rather than being happy for my success, she could only see trouble on the horizon. Naturally, she doesn't "get" blogs, much less Facebook or Twitter—"I don't need daily updates on my own life"—or any of the oversharing ways of the post-*Donahue* generation. And despite hearing about all the doors my blog was opening for me—one of my bosses at the *New York Times* even congratulated me when he saw my name on Page Six!—Mom remained convinced it was all going to blow up in my face, and ditto for the rest of the world that uses social media.

The basis for her doomsday theory? Her brother had been laid off from his job and had been struggling to find work around this time, and she swore no one would hire him because there was a *homosexual serial killer* by the same name who came up first when you searched her brother's name on Google—never mind the fact that the killer had been in prison since 1977. Who knows, though, Mom could end up being right. Around 1980, she predicted that the introduction of 401(k)s as a replacement to pensions would lead to the fleecing of the middle class, and I'd say she got that right. She's been calling this country's health insurance racket "legalized organized crime" for decades—well, until President Obama tried to do something about it. And with each new report of identity theft and breach of security via the Internet, she certainly seems to be living up to the Nostramomus nickname I gave her ... on my Facebook wall.

On a trip back to Arizona, my brother Bill, hoping to assuage her fears, all but forced her onto Facebook, setting up her profile and adding everyone she knew to her friends list, including the immediate family. This seemed like a good idea. She was constantly complaining about being left out of the loop, and couldn't even figure out how to download basic photo attachments that we were e-mailing her. But no sooner had she joined the social-media set than she removed me from her friends list because she found my frequent updates "annoying." While she adamantly denies unfriending me—"I don't even know what that means"—I know it wasn't my doing. Whatever the case, at no point did she ever write on my wall "Stop posting so frequently, *woman,*" so I considered this a small victory.

Cutting off contact with me on Facebook was probably just as well, though. Does anyone really want a parent to know every detail of his life? Besides, I had nearly severed all ties with Mom and my stepfather in the mid-'90s over another Web-related situation, when they insisted on referring to America Online as *American* Online, no matter how many times I corrected them. Exasperated, I pleaded with them to at least compromise and call it AOL, but to no avail.

These days, they no longer use America Online. And I do my best to overlook their insistence on continuing to use Yahoo.com as their home page. Still, Mom manages to get the better of me by calling my blog "Kenneth in the *Two-Twelve*."

My only solace comes from the fact that she, like everyone over sixty, is unable to get *American* Online to stop billing her $19.95 a month. I don't like seeing her get ripped off, but I figure it's a small price for the endless amount of pleasure this auto-bill payback brings me.

the thomas roberts affair

I arrived at the National Lesbian and Gay Journalists Association convention in San Diego over Labor Day weekend in 2007 as the representative for the *New York Times* and as the man behind one of the most popular new blogs. After years of anonymity, I was suddenly being recognized by lots of people—self-described "fans" who were telling me how much they loved my site—and the acknowledgment felt great.

The topic at the gathering quickly turned to news anchor Thomas Roberts, who had made a splash by attending the previous year's convention in Miami with his partner, Patrick. While Roberts, then an anchor on CNN's Headline News Network, had never been in the closet, his sexuality was brought into the spotlight for the first time when *Boston Globe* reporter Johnny Diaz wrote about his attendance at the conference on his blog, and the gays were going gaga about the possibility of a reappearance.

Like many newsmen before him, Roberts was best known for his leading-man looks, and the fact that he was gay only fanned the flame(r)s. As the gaggle of gays grew giddier with anticipation that Roberts might show up again, I remembered that a colleague of his from CNN had sent me some interesting pictures the previous summer, photos that were clearly shots of Roberts's naked torso/crotch and ass. His head may have been cropped off, but the body matched countless shirtless photos Roberts had posted elsewhere online. These pictures, I was told, had been used in a profile on a gay hookup site in Atlanta, where Roberts was based at CNN's headquarters.

With all of the gay journalists ooh-ing and aah-ing over the prospect of a Roberts repeat, I agreed that I'd love for him to show up in San Diego, then casually mentioned that I happened to have some explicit photos of him. If I had felt popular because of my blog, now I was vaulted to celebrity status, with literally dozens and dozens of guys clamoring to get to me as word of my scoop circulated. I didn't have a smartphone at the time, so at first I attempted to show some of the guys the photos on the computers they had set up in the conference's job expo, where I was running the *New York Times*' booth. My *Boston Globe* colleague Johnny Diaz would cover for me as I did my civic duty for my fellow gays. But the demand grew to be overwhelming—and the nature of the photos didn't really lend itself to a displaying in a crowded room—so I ended up setting up a "viewing area" in my hotel room, and watched in amazement as guys lined up all the way to the elevator for a peek at the headline news. If I'd been smart I'd have charged a cover.

One of the guys, who told me he was a good friend of Thomas's, was particularly amused by the whole situation, and asked me why I hadn't posted the photos on my blog yet. I kind of shrugged. My site was pretty PG at that point, and the idea had never really occurred to me. But the more we talked about it, the more insistent he became.

"You *have* to post these, Kenneth," he said. "I love Thomas, but if he's stupid enough to think he can put these on the Internet while he's on national television, he deserves to have them seen by everyone!"

I was ambivalent about the whole thing. I never saw it as him being deserving or not deserving of anything. I just knew the photos were sizzling hot, and I was quickly learning that my audience would totally enjoy seeing them. But the more I thought about it, the more I realized I had been giving Roberts a pass because he was "one of us," and I began to question whether this was right or not. I then asked myself what I would do if, say, Mark Steines from *Entertainment Tonight* had posted similar photos on a straight swingers site, or if Brian Williams had posted something on a daddy fetish site (a guy can dream), and the answer was clear: I'd post them. So I posted the Roberts photos.

What happened next was crazier than anything I had ever experienced, as media outlets from across the country picked up my not-so-blind item. I never named Thomas as the owner of the hot ass—or the black pussy ... cat also on the bed—but it was obvious who it was. Within days, the story was the lead item on the *New York Post*'s Page Six gossip page:

NEW SEX MESS JOLTS "INSIDER"

NOT even a week into his new gig at *The Insider,* former CNN Headline News anchor **Thomas Roberts** has brought yet another embarrassment to the syndicated Paramount TV show.

Yesterday, blogger **Kenneth Walsh** posted this question about the openly gay TV stud: "Which TV insider has been known to make his own headline news with these superhot nude pics of himself on the gay cruising site Manhunt.net?"

The photos on the site do not show the fellow's face, but the profile does feature pictures of a toe-tapper posing naked in various positions, including full frontal.

The Insider, a tabloid show known best for its round-the-clock coverage of Anna Nicole Smith's death and featuring carnival-like freaks during sweeps week, would not confirm or deny that the man in the photos is their new anchor.

A spokesperson for the show would not put us in touch with Roberts. When we asked about the risqué online profile, the rep told Page Six, "We have hired Thomas Roberts from CNN for his journalistic strengths and integrity. It is unfortunate that after four days on the job at *The Insider,* he has become a victim of this malicious personal attack."

This isn't the first time the program has had to deal with a sex issue— host **Pat O'Brien** went into rehab in 2005 after voice mails were leaked onto the Internet of him trying to coax a woman into a threesome by saying "Let's have [bleep]ing sex and drugs and just go crazy."

But the Roberts imbroglio might help ratings, at least with viewers who take a wide stance on moral issues. The show comes in third, in a virtual tie with *Access Hollywood,* behind *Entertainment Tonight* and *Inside Edition.*

Once it made Page Six, it went viral: from *New York* magazine and the *Atlanta Journal Constitution* to MTV's *Best Week Ever* and Gawker. GLAAD even got in on the action. While the boost in blog traffic was fast and furious, so was the backlash. The comments section on sites that wrote about what I had "done"—as well as, I might add, posting the traffic-generating photos—were aggressively hostile, either questioning how anyone could be sure it was him to claiming that Roberts's well-documented status as a survivor of sex abuse by a Roman Catholic priest made him an unfair target for such exposure. (Huh?)

An amateurish YouTube "editorial," a magazine article, and dozens of blog posts attacking me followed, as did a slew of anonymous death threats. While many of my friends expressed concern for my well-being—and several media outlets contacted me for comment—I thought the whole thing was ridiculous, so I opted to say nothing at all. I accepted that some people thought it was shitty of me to post the photos. I wasn't about to claim it was a nice thing to do, but I was comfortable with my decision. Thomas Roberts was a public figure and, as such, had forfeited his right to certain things. I hadn't stolen the photos or obtained them surreptitiously, so as far as I was concerned, the only person to blame for their being on the Internet—if "blame" needed to be assigned at all—was Roberts himself. And frankly, I didn't see any shame in him being caught flaunting his beautiful body.

Neither he nor any of his representatives ever contacted me.

Roberts was living in Los Angeles during this time, and he was now collecting a handsome paycheck working for a show that in short order was reporting extensively on nude photos of Disney star Vanessa Hudgens—taken when she was a minor—that were leaked on the Internet by an ex-boyfriend. The irony was not lost on anyone with half a brain.

Roberts eventually left *The Insider* and moved back to New York, and I spotted him at a National Lesbian and Gay Journalists Association cocktail party, but decided it was wise to steer clear of him. (I made a joking reference about the near run-in on my blog that night, captioning a photo: "Thomas Roberts is here—somebody call security!")

Three years went by. Then my friend Jay took me out to celebrate my birthday one night at a lounge in Chelsea. We'd been there only a few minutes when I felt someone tap me on the shoulder. When I turned, I wasn't sure what was happening. I hadn't had Lasik eye surgery yet, but I was too vain to wear my glasses in a gay venue, so my first thought was that it was my pal Ron Corning, who is also a news anchor. (It's the standard look: borderline perfection.) But when "Ron" didn't greet me with a smile or a hug, I realized it was someone far less happy to see me. I took a small step backward to get a better, far-sighted look at my visitor.

"Is that you, Thomas?" I asked, still truly uncertain if this

Kathy Griffin-Whitney Houston moment was actually about to go down.

With an "of course you know it's me" eye roll, Roberts asked if he could speak to me for a minute in private, motioning for me to follow him to an empty corner of the bar. I had always known this day might come, so I wasn't completely unprepared. And while I tend to hate confrontations, I was strangely at peace in the moment, ready for whatever was coming next. I would post those photos again in a minute, but I also recognized that my doing so had had ramifications for him. He clearly had been embarrassed and had agreed to a softball interview with *The Advocate* to try to put the whole thing behind him. (It was a low moment for *The Advocate*. The piece made *Parade* magazine look like hard-hitting journalism, as the reporter never once asked Roberts to confirm or deny that the photos were of him, nor did he ask any obvious follow-up questions to anything else.) So I had decided in advance that if Roberts ever confronted me, I would listen to whatever he wanted to say. As far as I was concerned I owed him that much.

This is what happened next:

Him (alcohol on his breath and standing about two inches away from my face): "I just wanted to say thank you."

Me: Silent, with the "I know you don't really mean that, so just get to what you really mean" expression on my face that people make when someone who wants to kill you says they just want to thank you.

Him: "I want to thank you for helping me address some really destructive behaviors in my life."

Me: Silent. I'm still not buying it, but not quite realizing the train is about to pull out of the station for Crazy Town.

Him: "So I should really thank you."

Me: "Um, OK."

Then the gears shifted:

Him: "But I just have to ask you something. Do you have any idea what you did to me? Do you have any idea?"

Me: Listening, looking him directly in the eye.

Him: "I have been lying in the fetal position for years because of what you did to me."

Me: Listening, kind of stunned that he was revealing this to me.

Him (his voice growing louder): "I had always appreciated the coverage you had given me, but then you wielded your power and used it against me."

Me: Getting increasingly concerned.

Him: "And I'll bet you just loved all the publicity it gave you, Kenneth. You loved every minute of it, didn't you? Just admit it."

Me: Still listening, but thinking, Um, yeah. Isn't that why people write blogs—so people will read them? Of course I loved the publicity, and my readers loved the pictures of your gorgeous body.

Him: "And do you know what the worst part of it is, Kenneth?"

Me: "No, what's that, Thomas?"

Him: "We were friends. We were peers, and we were friends. And then you went and did this. I just don't see how you could do that to a friend of yours."

Me (willing to let him have his say, but not willing to let him lie): "Thomas, I'm sorry if this hurt you, I really am. But let's be clear about something. We were not friends. We don't even know each other."

Thomas (indignantly): "What do you mean? Yes we were. There's even a picture of us together right there on your blog!"

Me (stunned that a famous person would confuse a "pic with" with an actual friendship; isn't that what stalkers do with celebrities, not the other way around?): "Thomas, seriously. You and I are not friends. I asked you to pose for that picture at an event a couple years ago, and so did a dozen other guys there. But be serious. We don't know each other, and we're certainly not friends. I have pictures with lots of famous people, and that doesn't mean I'm friends with any of them. I mean, really. I also have a picture with Debbie Gibson on there."

Him (incredulously): "Well, if you think you're friends with Debbie Gibson, then you're *delusional*!"

Me: 360-degree head spin. Did he actually just say that?

Him: "And I can't believe you wrote that about seeing me at that NLGJA fundraiser: 'Thomas Roberts is here—better call security!' Did you actually think that I would harm you? Do you think I'm a violent person?"

Me (sort of stunned that he was still reading my blog at all): "No, Thomas. I was just kidding around because it was the first time we'd seen each other since the incident. I thought it was kind of awkward, so I wrote that as a joke. I was just being sarcastic."

Him: "You were being sarcastic? Well, you didn't put it in parentheses."

Me (to myself): Oh, my God. It's as if William Hurt walked off the screen from *Broadcast News*. News anchors really do think like this. "No, Thomas, you're right. I didn't put that in parentheses. But I'm pretty sure my readers can tell when I'm being sarcastic."

He then proceeded to vent for another forty-five minutes, frequently alluding to the priest who had sexually abused him as a teen. He fluctuated between anger ("I've been imagining this moment for the last three years, and you're not acting anything like I expected you to; you're just standing there!") and forgiveness ("I just want to put this behind me. I don't want it to be uncomfortable when we see each other out at events. Can't we just hug this out?"). Physical contact was not something I was eager for (I don't even like to be touched when I'm having sex), but he wasn't going to take no for an answer. Suddenly, he put both of his arms around me, so I half-heartedly put my non-drink arm around him—thoroughly creeped out, not entirely sure he wasn't going to knee me, and wondering what he was capable of in his drunken state. My "hug" prompted him to say: "*Both* arms, Kenneth! Use *both* arms!"

One of his friends must have seen this bizarre display of "affection" so he came over—much to my relief—and I could sort of hear him saying that all their friends had left and he was planning to take off, too.

"That's enough, Thomas," his friend whispered, "I think that's enough."

Drunk, but not too drunk to sense that his remaining friend was growing impatient, Thomas turned to me as if we were old friends and said, "Hey. I'm gonna walk him out. Just wait right here." And then he was gone.

Feeling like the victim of a home invasion who has been instructed not to move or call the police until thirty minutes after the attacker has left, I sort of stood there alone, exactly where he left me, as my friend Jay and his two friends looked over at me in total disbelief. Jay's friends thought I had just been hit on by the hottest guy in the bar, while Jay wasn't entirely sure I hadn't just been *hit* by the hottest guy in the bar. It's a thin line between love and hate—no parentheses needed.

Checking to make sure the coast was clear, I finally rejoined my birthday posse and said the first thing that came into my head: "Did *that* really just happen?"

Jay, who knew the full backstory, was equally stunned, but he confessed that he'd been so taken aback that he'd neglected to film any of the action with his BlackBerry. (And he calls himself a friend.) Having already stayed out way past his bedtime while keeping a protective eye on me, Jay announced that he had to go.

I woke up the following day to find this e-mail message from him:

"I can't believe I had to leave after your Thomas Roberts *Housewives* reunion moment. I kept waiting for Andy Cohen to pop up with a fistful of cards and start reading blog-reader questions."

It was a surreal "conclusion" to the most scandalous moment in my blog's history, one that wouldn't end there.

Believing that alcohol had gotten in the way of actually putting this behind us, I sent Thomas an e-mail message shortly afterward, saying that I wanted him to know that I was sincerely sorry for any pain I had caused him. I reiterated what I had tried to tell him at the bar: that I'd have done the same thing if naked photos of any celebrity had exclusively come my way, and that I didn't post them to hurt him; I posted them because they were smoking hot! I also told him that hearing what he had to say did help me (as a blogger) to realize that there is a human being behind every fun scandal.

Rather than recognizing the sentiment behind my note, Roberts responded with a hostile message that still accepted no responsibility for posting the photos in the first place, and condemned me for not "really" apologizing and for making excuses for my "lapse in all judgment." Then about a year after he accosted me I read he got thrown out of a fancy-schmancy gay wedding at the Four Seasons for "causing a commotion" during Aretha Franklin's performance during the reception, then "argued with security before they ordered him to leave." (Towson, we have a problem—and it has nothing to do with me.)

And that's when I had a moment of clarity, when I realized why we were never going to see eye-to-eye on this: Celebrities, it seems, surround themselves with people who tell them only what they want to hear, and it was clearly eating at him that I was not willing to play that role. He reached out to me yet again after this, and I finally had to tell him enough is enough.

There must be people who are close to Mr. Anchorman who know that Thomas—and only Thomas—is to blame for this "lapse in all judgment." But none of them would ever dare tell him this, for fear of being pushed aside. When you're famous, every story you tell is fascinating, every joke you tell is hilarious, and every opinion you have is right. Still, I wish Thomas nothing but the best.

174

The irony of this whole situation is that if it had taken place a couple of years later—when everyone from reality stars to Academy-Award-winning actors deliberately "leak" naked photos online—Thomas might have thanked me for the added exposure, or even put me up to it. But it happened when these types of images still carried a stigma, so it's clear that he will continue to blame anyone but himself for what he did, and I can't say I'm all that surprised. Look at the example the Catholic Church set for him so many years ago.

don't you hear what i hear?

I received some unexpected good news for my legal team recently.

Joyce Cohen of the *New York Times* has presented a compelling defense strategy for when I finally snap and murder one or more of the following type of people:

That jackass who insisted on bringing a block of cheese and a box of Carr's Table Water crackers to work every week, and then proceeded to rattle the packaging on both nonstop during his nine-hour appetizer course that he calls "work." (My shift was only seven hours, but I'm fairly certain this went on for at least nine.)

The arrogant prick who insists on humming on the subway platform every day, because we all must love to listen to *whatever* noise he wants to make.

The dick at the DMV whose nose whistled like a goddamn choo-choo train that is about to approach me but will never pass.

The self-aware-less colleague who brought a bottomless cup of ice to his desk each night at work and crunched every last cube in it. (Allow two to three hours for this to run its course.)

The "jock" on the treadmill at the gym who whistled during his entire (attempted) thirty-minute run. (You're lucky I limited myself to merely pulling the emergency stop button on your machine.)

The assortment of assholes at the park who think they are brightening everyone's day by mindlessly half-singing a happy tune.

Mr. and Mrs. Fuckface, who brought a lifetime supply of pistachios to the movies, then sat directly beside me in the back row—in a theater that was ninety-five percent empty—clicking the shells and crunching on the nuts, then tossing the remains on the floor. (It didn't help that this happened after a woman took not one but *three* phone calls in a crowded movie theater the night before. It wasn't until the third call that someone finally had the good sense to scream, "Get the fuck off the phone!"—as if you should have to tell anyone that in a movie theater.)

The "healthy eater" who brought a salad to work every day in a Rubbermaid storage container, then poured the dressing on at her desk, put the lid back on and shook and shook and shook and shook and shook the salad—gotta make sure that dressing's evenly distributed—to the point that I had to leave the newsroom each day at 1:30 p.m. and go downstairs to cool off.

While I may not be able to avoid criminal charges entirely, surely a jury of my peers would let me off easy if they knew that I suffered from misophonia, a condition I didn't even know had a name—even though I had a severe case of it—until Cohen's "When a Chomp or a Slurp Is a Trigger for Outrage" appeared in the paper. It quickly became the paper's most e-mailed article that day, although I'm pretty sure that was only because everyone I've ever known sent it to me.

In it, Cohen wrote:

For people with a condition that some scientists call misophonia, mealtime can be torture. The sounds of other people eating—chewing, chomping, slurping, gurgling—can send them into an instantaneous blood-boiling rage.

Uh-huh.

She continued:

Many people can be driven to distraction by certain small sounds that do not seem to bother others—gum chewing, footsteps, humming. But sufferers of misophonia, a newly recognized condition that remains little studied and poorly misunderstood, take the problem to a higher level.

To my amazement this complete stranger was describing my life for the past thirty years. When she said this condition was frequently linked to anxiety disorders, I began to involuntarily nod my head over and over, in a way that surely would have annoyed me if someone else were doing it. Overwhelmed by my discovery, I began searching for more information, leading me first to the Wikipedia entry, which also appeared to have been based on my life:

> Misophonia, literally "hatred of sound," is a form of decreased sound tolerance. It is a neurological disorder characterized by negative experiences resulting only from specific sounds, whether loud or soft, and is often used interchangeably with the term Selective Sound Sensitivity.

> Symptoms: People who have misophonia are most commonly annoyed, or even enraged, by such ordinary sounds as other people eating, breathing, sniffing, or coughing; certain consonants; or repetitive sounds. People with misophonia may be diagnosed with mood or anxiety disorders as well as obsessive-compulsive disorder. Though a few sufferers are bothered by sounds they make themselves, most are not. The reactions are completely involuntary.

This revelation felt just like when I discovered what it meant to be gay, only with far more unwanted oral action. For years I have sat in not-so-silent rage—muttering things like "Stop it!" and "Shut the fuck up!" under my breath, which I've since learned through misophonia message boards is a common outlet—around certain coworkers, only to have others tell me they had no idea what I was talking about, or that I was being ridiculous.

At one of my old jobs, I'd complain to my colleague friends about a gruff former college football player who battled his nicotine addiction by repeatedly stuffing pieces of gum into his mouth and nervously—and very, very loudly—chomping on them for hours on end until the wad was the size of a racquetball, expecting them to commiserate with me. Instead, I'd be greeted with blank stares—or worse.

"What do you mean? I didn't even notice he was doing that," they would say, looking completely bewildered, as if I were making this up, even though they had also been sitting right next to the offending colleague. Or, "How do you even *notice* that?"

(Getting them on board with my outrage about another coworker's insistence on asking everyone in the newsroom if they would like to join her "in a spot of tea," then proceeding to place five tea bags and water into her Mrs. Tea machine, an asinine invention if ever there was one—teabag + hot water = cup of tea; absolutely no "machine" is required—that serves no purpose other than to make extremely annoying gurgling noises for hours on end, proved to be an even tougher sell.)

The message was clear and consistent: *I* was the one with the problem—and possibly had the best hearing since Jaime Sommers's right ear hit the air in 1975.

I was relieved to finally have a name for my condition, so I posted Cohen's article on my Facebook wall thinking I would finally be afforded some compassion. Ha! The pushback was hostile and instantaneous, like a public nail clipper at a misophonia convention.

"Sounds like someone needs to take a Chill-the-Fuck-Out pill," wrote one "friend."

"Every malady has a name these days," wrote another, the eye-roll clear.

"My sister has this, too: But we call it Get the Fuck Over Yourself Syndrome," was the last comment before I deleted the post.

But despite the outpouring of "support" from my friends, I was comforted by the article's backing my belief that my reactions were indeed completely involuntary. (And by the way, so are the vicious names I use to refer to these people— or at least that's what I've decided.) So it was a relief to know I wasn't crazy and I wasn't alone, but what could I do about it? I saw the name of a renowned audiologist in the *Times* article, so I reached out to her directly.

"Does an eight-year-old wake up and say, 'Today my dad's eating cereal is going to drive me insane? Of course not," Marsha Johnson immediately said to me on the phone, all but laughing at how ridiculous it is to think misophonia sufferers could control this if they really wanted to. Johnson is an audiologist in Portland, Oregon, who along with eleven colleagues helps set the Misophonia Management Protocol for therapists across the country.

"This process is much more complex, and I know it's been reduced to a couple of sentences. But I think these people who have it would really like to have a better understanding. It's been a real process of definition."

Like the neuroscientist interviewed in the *Times* piece, Dr. Johnson agrees that misophonia is probably not an auditory disorder at all.

"I think it's a central nervous system problem," she said. "It's a question of physiology."

While there is no cure for misophonia, Dr. Johnson told me that her patients tend to be smart people who know themselves well and rearrange their lives around the disorder—like when I took a ride on the elevator while my former colleague prepared her salads, obvious victims of Shaken Baby Lettuce Syndrome.

She said misophonics also tend to pick careers where they are less likely to be "working in a roomful of people eating Cheetos," often gravitating toward jobs where they are able to work from home.

But despite my best efforts to avoid high-annoyance situations, they're like landmines in Angola, and Princess Diana isn't around to help anymore. And newsrooms happen to be packed with people who are both smart *and* prone to eating out of vending machines. Many copy desks have seven-hour shifts, so leaving the office to get food is difficult, and eating at desks is common. But that's not even the half of it.

Some people bring food from home, like the guy who brought two apples to work every day and incessantly chomped on them all night—staring at them in between bites, so proud of his healthy snack—and then smugly chucked the core in the trash when he'd had enough. (I'm still waiting for the *Times* article on the condition where people cannot tolerate when people discard food trash in wastepaper baskets rather than kitchen containers where it belongs. I have an acute case of that, too.)

Not to mention the "sports guy" who used to help out on my old desk. From what I could gather, he would stop at the supermarket and load up two carts before coming to work each day, then unload his groceries at his desk: a two-liter bottle of Pepsi, a family-size bag of tortilla chips, a jar of mild salsa, two sandwiches, two yogurts, and a fruit basket to snack on in between meals, occasionally taking a break from eating to edit a story. It was a cacophony of annoyance.

And don't forget about the "RSI guy" with the "ergonomic" keyboard that emitted a special brand of clicking. (Oh, that clicking.) If he really needed it, it would be one thing. But once it got to be too much trouble for him to set up every day—many copy editors share desks, so he wasn't allowed to leave it there after his shift—he stopped even bothering to haul it out anymore. Thanks for the memories, dumb-ass.

While it may be true that most of these people have no idea they are bothering me, it doesn't make the level of irritation any less severe. And in most cases, they are doing things that anyone with any sense of common decency would know not to do in the first place, like this fairly recent incident: I was at work when I suddenly could hear nothing but a woman in a neighboring department sitting across from me popping and cracking her gum, each jaw movement more ferocious than the last. I was in a "slot" position—copy-editor jargon for being in a position of authority—so I could not simply get up from my desk, but the sound became increasingly overwhelming. I started to think I was on a hidden-camera show—this woman is easily sixty years old, yet she's chomping on her gum like an excited eight-year-old at her first trip to the Magic Kingdom?—but no one from the Funt family ever came forward. Nearing an explosion, I leaned over to another colleague to ask her if I was "being ridiculous." This man, who normally is able to tune out everything and laughs at me when I complain about others, immediately assured me I was not, which instead of making me feel less alone managed to enrage me even more. (Even *Bob* noticed!) I tried to regain my composure and refocus on my work, but my blood started boiling, and then everything went blurry.

Before I knew it—and before I had even thought about how I might go about this diplomatically—I was suddenly standing, and leaning over the monitor in the direction of Miss Big League Chew. My right arm suddenly raised itself, and my index finger started pointing in her direction in a slow and deliberate circular motion, like a drag queen might while preparing to size you up before making you wish you'd never stepped into this particular filthy gay bar.

It's not unusual for our desks to speak to each other about a story, so she looked up at my pointing self, clearly anticipating my asking her something about whatever was in the news. Instead, a bizarrely calm and sincere voice that I didn't even know existed inside me took control of my mouth and calmly said, "Hey. Could you please not pop your gum?"

Stunned, she sheepishly replied, "Oh, sure. I'm sorry about that."

I said, "Thanks," and sat back down—I was seeing stars by now, and my ears were ringing—completely in shock that being direct and polite had actually worked and wondering what this said about my strict lifelong policy of passive-aggressive behavior.

But I knew in my heart that I got lucky in that particular instance. I had tried to speak to my former boss about a colleague's bizarre throat-clearing habit, but instead of sympathizing, she got testy and finally snapped, "Well, what exactly do you want *me* to do about it?"

I relayed this information to Dr. Johnson and sure enough, she confirmed my suspicion that one of the biggest challenges in misophonia treatment is the hostile reaction sufferers receive when confronting people who are the source of what she calls "triggers."

That's when Dr. Johnson told me about her most successful treatment options. Since 1997, when she saw her first case, about eighty-five percent of her patients have seen "marked improvement" when they use hearing-aid-like devices that emit broadband noise, formerly called white noise, that block out just enough of the high-pitched sounds that tend to irritate misophonics.

I was intrigued. Friends have often suggested I listen to my iPod to drown out the offending sounds, but not only do I think that's unprofessional, I actually need to be able to hear what my colleagues are saying and doing. It's a newsroom, after all, and things are changing; news is breaking every second.

Armed with my new information, I began to feel slightly more hopeful that I would never actually kill someone and need to use the "misophonia defense" in a court of law. Dr. Johnson says the white-noise headphones not only work great; they often lead people to believe you're hard of hearing, which can garner the sympathy I have been longing for. (I'll take it any way I can get it, as long as they don't use that annoying baby voice that I just cannot stand the sound of.)

She also told me that natural relief was on the horizon— in the form of hearing loss. While she wasn't quite ready to advocate deliberately damaging my eardrums now, she did say that as we get older, our hearing tends to get worse. As a result, she said, she rarely sees clients who are in their fifties and sixties.

As we were getting ready to say our good-byes, I told Dr. Johnson I was willing to give the device a try—and that for the first time in my life, I was suddenly looking forward to getting old and going deaf. If all else fails, though, perhaps I will be able to get a soundproof cubicle built for me at my next job. While this may sound as crazy as wanting to punch someone for humming a happy tune, it may not be. Dr. Johnson says misophonia is now officially recognized by the U.S. government, under the Americans With Disabilities Act.

mulling martin

After getting a refresher course one afternoon on *Oprah* on just how adorable Ricky Martin was, I found myself more excited than I thought I would be to attend a book signing for the Latin superstar's coming-out memoir, *Me.* (Or *Yo,* for my Spanish readers.) My pal Daryl was in charge of these events at the Borders in the Time Warner Center and was forever hooking me up to meet and greet a host of celebrities who were in town to promote their latest books or albums. It was a guaranteed "pic with" for my blog—and often my friend could get me a private meet 'n' greet—so even though I wasn't a huge fan of Ricky's music, I wasn't about to miss the chance to meet one of the most famous and sexiest guys on the planet.

The morning of the event, I was told Ricky was doing no meet 'n' greets. I wasn't that surprised—the caliber of stars who usually pass through there was more along the lines of Belinda Carlisle, Kathy Griffin, and the two remaining gals from Bananarama—and I knew Daryl would still do whatever he could to hook me up. When I got there, I was immediately given a VIP bracelet—*Gracias, amigo!*—and told to wait with a small group of people inside the velvet rope near the stage, way ahead of the massive line that wrapped throughout the dying retail behemoth. I believe some of the VIPs had won their places at the front of the line through a radio contest, but quite a few others were disabled, and were given a special place to accommodate their needs.

While waiting for Ricky to arrive, I had befriended a young Latino named Jorge. Jorge used one of those walkers on wheels to help him get around, and at one point he asked me to tie his shoe for him ("Really tight, or else my foot will slip out of my shoe"). I was somewhat taken aback by his request at first—no one over the age of five had ever asked me to do that before—but obliged, assuming it was a struggle for him to do by himself, although it occurred to me that it would be funny if he'd asked me to do it just to fuck with me.

From there, we hit it off, talking about the *Oprah* appearance, our jobs, gay life in the Bronx (his home) versus Manhattan (mine), and agreeing that Ricky should dump his boyfriend and consider one of us. Sure, there were children involved. But Matteo and Valentino would adjust to their new stepfather, we figured. Kids are very resilient at that age.

When Ricky arrived, the place went absolutely wild. I wasn't thrilled with the knit hat—who hides hair *that* gorgeous?—but couldn't help but marvel at his beauty. Then, after posing for the throng of paparazzi near the front of the room for a few minutes, Ricky noticed some of his special-needs fans and immediately made a beeline to them. He took some extra time to chat with them and their families while signing their books.

Borders had announced that there would be absolutely NO PHOTOS at the signing table—the staff even had baskets where they were making people put their phones and cameras *before* approaching Señor Martin, but they seemed to look the other way when a special-needs VIP snapped a shot or two.

After a while, though, I started to get antsy. Ricky had been down on his knees catering to the wheelchair crowd for what seemed like forever, and I could see my new friend was getting concerned that he might not get any one-on-one time with his idol. Poor Jorge, I thought. Despite not being able to walk on his own, it was beginning to look as if he wasn't even disabled *enough* to get a little extra Latin lovin'. But just when it seemed all hope was lost, Ricky came over to us, the last of the VIPs, and greeted Jorge with a huge smile and a big hello. Jorge played it cool, although I'm sure he was about to die inside, and it was incredibly sweet seeing Ricky interact so caringly with his fans, making each one feel as special as the next.

Jorge—whose self-awareness I began to realize was as disabled as his legs—proceeded to talk Ricky's ear off, going on and on and on about the other time they had met ("Don't you remember?") and telling him how much he loved his new book (he already had a copy, "in both languages"), his new album, and what he thought of the previous album and something he'd said on *Oprah*. The fact that hundreds of other fans had been waiting in line for hours didn't seem to inhibit him at all and to be honest, I was kind of in awe. While no one has ever accused me of being unselfish, I'm the worst kind of self-centered: passive-aggressive. I'm too timid to ask for what I want—"Oh, the waiter's too busy to bring the check, I don't want to bother him"—yet I will complain endlessly when things don't go precisely my way ("I shouldn't *have* to ask for the bill—it's *obvious* I want to leave"), and I found Jorge's self-assuredness inspiring. Jorge then got me to take a handful of photos of him with Ricky, and then the singer began to prepare for the book signing in earnest.

Just at that moment, a member of the Borders security staff pulled me aside and said, "Excuse me, sir. Have all of *your people* gotten everything they need?"

Unsure what he meant at first, I quickly realized that somehow in all the excitement, the people running the line had gotten the impression that I was some sort of liaison for the disabled contingency there. I got so caught up in the moment that without even missing a beat, I turned around and began taking inventory of "my kids."

As God is my witness, a clipboard suddenly appeared in my hands.

Lorna in the electric wheelchair? Photo and autograph—check. Jessica in the old-school manual chair? She's good with just saying hello. Brad with the March of Dimes walking canes? All smiles. After I checked in on everyone—well, everyone except the woman with no lower body who had already monopolized Ricky's attention more flagrantly than even Jorge had—I finally gave the security guy the thumbs-up signal that, indeed, all *my kids* were good. (Interesting footnote: People with special needs love disposable cameras.)

But this act of selflessness came at a price. I realized I had neglected to get a picture with Ricky for myself, even though he had been standing about an inch away from me for twenty minutes. Truth is, I was so touched by everything that was going on that I focused entirely on helping Jorge and the others get the photos and autographs they wanted. (Jorge had actually bought a stack of books in Spanish for friends and family.) Still, once I realized the error of my selfless ways, I began to panic. I'd actually snuck out of a new job during an unscheduled "break"—and I needed something to show for it in case I got fired upon my return.

Now, with all of the special-needs VIPs taken care of, I was told that I was first in line, as I was a VIP in my own right by way of my friend Daryl. I approached the table ready for my big moment with Mr. Menudo, reaching out my hand as I told him my name (I couldn't think of a thing to say—I'm no good at this stuff no matter how many times I do it). He smiled and started signing my book, at which point I told him that they were not allowing us to take pictures, but that I'd really like one. (Security hadn't confiscated my camera because I was the "special-needs liaison.")

He looked me in the eye and said, "Go for it!" as he handed me my book. Naturally, I meant a photo *with* him— not just of him—but it was hard to be demanding with so many people waiting, so I snapped one. As I was getting ready to exit stage left, Ricky jumped back out from behind the table to talk to a recent arrival special-needs VIP. Nervous, but inspired by Jorge and sensing a second chance, I motioned for my friend Daryl (who had all but disappeared up until this moment) to come closer.

I whispered that I'd *love* to try to sneak a photo with Ricky—to which he replied: "You're not in a *wheelchair,*

Kenneth." Still, ever the good sport, Daryl waited there with me for our moment. Just as Ricky finished talking to his latest admirer, I discreetly asked him for a picture.

Ricky was halfway back on stage, but he graciously stopped and bent down to pose with me—don't ask me how, but I swear I put my hand on his chest and began rubbing— but for some reason Daryl and my camera weren't connecting. After what felt like ten minutes, Ricky finally gave up and turned around to go to the table and sign some books. (I don't think he was sure if the picture was taken, but I was certain he could tell I had two working legs.) Just as he did, the flash popped.

Naturally, I was bummed that the photo op had failed. But I was puzzled I wasn't feeling more disappointed about it. Ricky—a superstar who could have easily phoned in his appearance—brought a lot of joy to a lot of people that afternoon, I finally concluded, and it felt good knowing that I had helped facilitate it in some small way. My altruism had been purely accidental, but while I was reminded that it pays to ask for what you want, sometimes the things you don't ask for can be even more rewarding.

wasn't tomorrow wonderful?

If my unmitigated envy of Buffy and Jody's life in a high-rise apartment sparked my initial desire to move to New York back in grade school, it was Andy Warhol and his legion of Superstars and sycophants at the Factory that had me all but packing my bags by high school.

Between reading about his exploits with the-beautiful-and-the-damned heiress Edie Sedgwick in the '60s, and those endless nights with Truman and Liza and Bianca at Studio 54 in the '70s, I was convinced New York City held something magical for me. And by the time I reached my confused teen years in the early '80s, when the city's downtown scene exploded and Diane Brill seemed to rule the night, I knew that the only way I could survive the horrible "secret" inside me was to head east and become one of "Andy's Babies."

It's not that I was even a huge admirer of his work. Like most people, I got a kick out of his iconic Campbell's Soup and Jackie and Marilyn paintings. But I was hardly a die-hard fan. And it obviously wasn't a physical attraction, although by college I, like Edie, certainly didn't shy away from emulating his bizarre translucent appearance and white hair. Perhaps it's needless to say, but I was the only teenager wearing a black turtleneck on those scorching Phoenix afternoons back in the day.

What drew me to Andy Warhol was that he seemed like such a freak—just as I felt like one—yet he was still able to be successful and famous, and he had an unrivaled ability to attract the most beautiful, interesting, and talented people in the world to surround him. It was almost as if I wanted to see if he would accept me (whatever it was that *I* was; I wasn't even sure), because if he did, then maybe that meant I was OK after all.

The fact that my blond(i)e obsession—Debbie Harry, about whom I'd written two adoring essays in junior high school and whose photos covered every inch of my bedroom walls—seemed to be with him every time I picked up a magazine only made me more convinced that New York was the place for me. And that shortly after my arrival, we'd all become lifelong friends. If those new chicks Cyndi and Madonna wanted to join us, so much the better.

I'd also seen Debbie and Andy palling around on his new MTV show, *Andy Warhol's 15 Minutes.* My favorite episode was when he had the Brit boys Curiosity Killed the Cat on, and he could hardly keep himself from gushing all over 'em. That they used him in their "Misfit" video still makes me happy every time I watch it.

But no sooner had I completed my first semester of j-school—with all postgrad roads leading to New York and landing my dream job at *Interview* magazine—than we got the horrible news that Andy had died, following routine gallbladder surgery at New York Hospital. I was sitting on a stool at Graffiti's nightclub on Mill Avenue in Old Town Tempe with my friend Chantal, and we both were in utter shock. In the next few days, I combed papers for news of the funeral, spotting a picture of Stephen Sprouse and Debbie Harry in the *New York Times* arriving at Andy's memorial service at St. Patrick's Cathedral.

As the world began to mourn the death of an artistic icon, I began to mourn the death of a dream. Had Manhattan nightlife been changed forever? Would people ever go out again? Would *Interview* fold? All of my hopes seemed to die that day, as the New York scene I longed to be a part of suddenly seemed to be over before I even got there.

As the '80s came to a close, *The Andy Warhol Diaries* was published, and I raced to get a copy. By then, I had my first boyfriend and had come to realize I was not the only gay person in the world after all—or even in Phoenix. But I realized that even post-Warhol, my hunger for New York was as voracious as ever. Instead of reading the book from beginning to end, I naturally parked in the index pages and looked up every reference to my favorite stars: Maxwell Caulfield? YES! Bjorn Borg? YES! Jon-Erik Hexum? NO!— they'd obviously never met or else he'd have his own chapter! Of course, the entries about Debbie Harry were the first ones I read, and although I was tickled to hear intimate little details about their relationship, I began to learn that these enviable high-profile "friendships" were often not what they appeared:

> "Debbie isn't really interesting to talk to, but her interviews always come out right." (Page 402.)
> "If you saw [Debbie Harry and Chris Stein's] apartment ... it's so junky." (Page 298.)
> "Debbie's so fat now." (Page 457.)

Meow. This dead kitty had claws.

Shortly thereafter, I read former *Interview* editor Bob Colacello's eye-opening Warhol tell-all, *Holy Terror,* and learned more about what a manipulative, self-absorbed slave driver Andy had supposedly been. Nearly a decade later, when I had finally "made it" to New York, I introduced myself to Bob at a party at some polo club in the Hamptons and told him how as a kid, I'd dreamed of working for him, what a fan I was of his book, and how it had toughened me up for my career in publishing. He laughed and told me that it was funny that I should mention the book because he had just been contacted by "some kids" who were starting a new imprint and wanted to reissue *Holy Terror.* It was my "Factory" moment.

Although my bubble had been burst—Andy and Debbie really weren't best friends after all, and working at *Interview* was likely more of a nightmare than a dream—it probably wasn't such a bad thing. I don't want to say that it pre-jaded me for my future life in Los Angeles and New York. But it was probably just as well that when I first left home and landed on Santa Monica Boulevard at age twenty-two, I was not as completely naïve to the ways of the world as I might have been otherwise—fresh from Mesa, living at home, and watching *Family Ties* and *The Cosby Show* with the family every week.

Although I let my beloved subscription to *Interview* lapse years ago, I still smile when I go back and flip through Andy's diaries, since they remind me of a completely different place in my life and the world.

With Andy dead more than twenty-five years now and Debbie far older than he was when he died (and increasingly spending her time at her home in New Jersey) it can sometimes seem as if that whole era was just a dream. But for me, the dream lives on. People kept telling me that my whole life wouldn't change just because I moved to New York, but it completely did. It's like when my friend Carolyn wanted a nose job. Everyone said she shouldn't put too much importance in that—"You'll still be the same person once it's done," they cautioned—but her life really did change overnight. She was finally able to land modeling gigs and move to Milan, and she never looked back. New York City was my nose job.

In a twist that I could never have anticipated, I ended up getting invited to a one-night-only reopening of Studio 54 in late 2011. Legendary party promoter Chip Duckett was kind enough to include Michael and me. Everyone associated with the notorious den of iniquity played a part in this historic special event: Former co-owner Ian Schrager (now a wildly successful hotelier) was there, as well as the club's original entertainment producer, doorman, DJs, and bartender Scott Taylor. Even the late Steve Rubell's former assistant Myra Scheer was on hand, wisely making no comments about taxes.

The second Michael, my friend Scooter LaForge, and I arrived on West 54th Street, all three of us got chills. Gawkers

and limos were littering the
celebrities from the A- to Z-list w
in reliving a part of New York Ci

Once we got through the v
used a friend like Chip back in t
as if we'd been transported
Bianca?"), as gorgeous young
nothing but short shorts and tube socks, ౼౼
every whim. (Well, *almost* every whim.)

Feeling a tad overwhelmed, we snuck upstairs to catch
our breath and take in the whole thing. It was kind of awe-
inspiring to think of all the famous people who had partied in
these hallowed halls before us—Michael (when he was black),
Liz, Warren, Diane, Salvador, Brooke, Woody, Olivia—and
all the nights of decadence with Truman and Andy and
Halston and Liza. And this was also where director Stanley
Dorfman shot Blondie's "Heart of Glass" video!

We began to spot some bold-faced names. Kevin Bacon
and a parade of the *beautiful people* were within earshot in a
VIP section. And then it wasn't long before we began to run
into some other familiar faces, including my pal Jeffrey, who
regaled us with stories of Divine and Bianca and Calvin
during his brief stint as a Studio 54 bartender in the late '70s.
(Jeff would later do home-design work for Calvin.)

The photo op of the evening for Michael—who almost
never does "pic-withs"—was meeting legendary 1970s New
York Knickerbocker Walt "Clyde" Frazier, who was as cool
as they come. I, on the other hand, went for another legendary
'70s "athlete": Rollerina, who returned to the stage as if thirty
years had never skated by.

But then it was back to the main floor, which felt like
arriving at the Promised Land: And there it was, hanging
above the dance floor: The Moon and the Spoon! Just my
luck, I was hanging out with a recovered cocaine addict; it
was going to have to be a vodka night, open bar courtesy of
Stoli.

Siano and Leroy Washington had the place in a
esday night fever—Donna Summer's "MacArthur
e Village People's "San Francisco," Vicki Sue
on's "Turn the Beat Around"—but it wasn't until Diana
's "The Boss" came pumping through the speakers that
ichael and I had no choice but to dance. (It's my favorite
disco song of all time—if not my favorite song, period.)

As we moved around the famous dance floor, I couldn't help
but smile and bask in the moment, realizing that I was dancing at
the Studio 54—and that most of my craziest childhood dreams
had actually come true. I had built an incredible life for myself in
New York City, with a cozy home, great friends, and a sweet guy.
I had a loving and supportive family. I had gotten to work at some
of the most prestigious news organizations in the world. And I had
even managed to carve out a small niche for myself in the
crowded world of New York media, through which I have been
fortunate to have met some of the most interesting actors,
musicians, athletes, journalists, and writers of our day—and a few
of my childhood heroes—including Debbie Harry, Paul Weller,
Roger Federer, Novak Djokovic, Billie Jean King, Barney Frank,
Matt Lauer, Tina Brown, Dan Rather, Walter Cronkite, Jane
Pauley, Dustin Lance Black, Edward Burns, Rosanne Cash, Lisa
Kudrow, Ronnie Spector, *The Daily Show* co-creator Lizz
Winstead, and countless others.

Even more remarkable, I thought, is that I lived to see things
change monumentally for LGBT people, something I never
imagined I'd be around for. While my right-leaning friends and
relatives use barely masked racism to pick President Obama apart,
even many of my most liberal cohorts never miss a chance to
point out what a disappointment he's been, and how he "wasted"
such an enormous opportunity for true change. But I couldn't
disagree more. He may be George W. Bush 2.0 in many areas of
foreign policy and national security. But he is also the shrewd
architect of the last great civil rights movement of our lifetime.
Attitudes trickle down from the top. And with President Obama
repeatedly standing up to the nation—and the world—and saying

LGBT people are equal in every way, I now feel for the first time that my life is truly valid. You can run away to more accepting places and surround yourself with supportive people all you want. But until your government stops telling you that you are less than, and revokes laws designed to humiliate and demean you, the feeling of self-loathing does not go away. No one, liberal or conservative, should underestimate what this president's actions have done for so many.

But then, after all that dancing, we decided it was time to head back upstairs to the mezzanine, where I got to hang out with Chip—he *finally* wasn't working at an event we were both at—his pal Fred Schneider of the B-52's, and some young Broadway hunk.

And then, just like that, the entire evening shifted gears, as fifty of the most handsome young men you've ever seen— like Noah's Ark for singles—started to flood the joint. It was *sooo* Studio 54. I quickly noticed they were *Cosmo* Bachelor of the Year contestants. I approached Mr. Colorado and asked him if a winner had been named yet. The hunk seemed a little stunned that I knew what all the hoopla was about, until I explained that "*Cosmo* Bachelor of the Year" T-shirts were kind of a giveaway. (Somebody call Calvin, we've got a live one!) Mr. Colorado politely told me that, as a matter of fact, the winner had been announced just minutes earlier: Mr. Ohio.

And then, right on cue, Mr. Ohio, a twenty-eight-year-old entertainment reporter from Cleveland, appeared before my eyes. He was a knockout, all right, and he smiled as I recounted memories of going to Cedar Point—a famous amusement park in Sandusky, Ohio—as a kid growing up in Detroit.

Suddenly, we were meeting corn-fed bachelors left and right. Mr. Virginia was very sweet and personable (he was an aspiring singer), Mr. North Dakota was surprised I had some history in Minot (my grandmother from Omaha, Nebraska, took a job there in the 1950s—"Why not Minot?"), and he introduced me to Mr. Nebraska, with whom he went to school in Lincoln. Mr. New York—as only a New Yorker would— hesitated about having his picture taken. ("What's it for?")

Meeting all the guys had me thinking the voting was spot-on until Mr. Michigan walked into the room—and I all but demanded a recount on the spot.

Mr. Michigan, a twenty-six-year-old who told me he was from Flint, was without question the hottest guy in the bunch. Tall, friendly, and personable—just how I like my studs. This night couldn't be any more perfect.

By then, Michael, Scooter, and even Chip were ready to call it a night. But since I didn't have to be at work until the following afternoon, I stuck around for just one more drink. As I got it, I ran into former bartender Jeffrey, who continued to delight me with stories of Studio 54 of old, and we danced some more before calling it a night. Part of me wanted to go straight home and document every second of the evening— *Andy Warhol Diaries*-style—but I was too drunk and was feeling emotional because it was over all too soon. In a way, I had been waiting my entire life for this night. All the dances and proms I didn't get to go to, all of the New Year's Eves and Valentine's Days I didn't get to truly be a part of all seemed to fade away. I was "on the list" at Studio 54, and for a brief moment, nothing else seemed to matter. Tomorrow actually was as wonderful as I'd always dreamed it would be.

As I got out of the cab near my apartment, I realized I had been so excited in the hours leading up to the event that I hadn't eaten a proper dinner. So instead, I bought a huge Drake's coffee cake and a pint of Häagen-Dazs Chocolate Peanut Butter ice cream at the corner bodega and stumbled up the stairs home. After devouring the Drake's cake—for those not from the East, it's like an entire *box* of Hostess Crumb Cakes all rolled into one—I opened the ice cream, which was too frozen for the spoon to make any headway. Undeterred, I sank my entire upper jaw directly into the container, and ate every last bite before passing out, at long last a bona fide New Yorker, just like the neurotic characters in the Woody Allen movies I had been obsessed with since I was a boy.

Liza would have been proud.

acknowledgments

I am grateful to so many people, most notably Bernard Michael Smith, my lover and partner in crime, who patiently talked me off a ledge on more occasions than I care to recall; Mark LeGault, for being such a loyal friend and always being my biggest fan; Greg Jelinek, for never failing to make me laugh; Lynn Hoogenboom, for her big heart and eager willingness to help; Leah Zibulsky, for cracking me up and then cracking the whip; Carol Carney, Dr. Sharon Bramlett, and Sherrie Good, for all seeing something in me early on; Christopher Carozzo, for his many hours of research and encouragement; Mike Wood, for taking a chance on me and publishing my first essay; the late David Rakoff, for his parting words of encouragement; Chris Butler, whose way with words made me want to try; and Don Weise, my editor, for "getting it," and championing this project from the start.

And to my family, without whom most of these stories would not be possible. Mom: You're my favorite. I love you more than you know; Gary: Thanks for surprising me and becoming the father that I thought I'd never have; Bill: You may have led us down this path, but it's been a fun journey because of you; Terence: You're the most hilarious person I know—and thank God you remember everything, so I didn't have to think I was making half of this up; and Jennifer: You're the sweetest, most thoughtful person in my life. I was right to be so happy the day they brought you home. And what a wonderful mother you've turned out to be.

Also want to thank the following people for their enduring friendship and/or support: Nina Kuzniak, Ken Headley, Jay Shows, Mary Reid, Jean Arnold, Kandy Studzinski Gilligan, Paula Bohan O'Brien, Kristen Giddens Pinto-Coelho, Donna Rutkowski, Francine Ruley, Kristen Casteleiro, Lois Dei, Sue Bazarewski, Mary Carew, Scooter LaForge, Frank Anthony Polito, Craig Bentley, Marc Lallanilla, Mary Armstrong, Jesse Mayshark, Ray Krueger, Mike Kelley, Lois Stuart, Debra Pasquerette, Yuki Laubmeier, Deanna Johnson, Christina Morrison, Kurt Davidson, Matt Noonan, Bill Rickman, Kelly Fitzmaurice, Seimond London, Alisa Gumbs, Greg Gregor, Kevin Fleck, Matt D'Amico, Keith Eby, Tony Goldsberry, Chad Townsend, Scott Prendergast, Chip Duckett, Jeff Isaacs, Benny Gonzalez, Joe Melvin, Yogita Patel, John and Nina Richter, Matthew Rettenmund, David Mixner, Kevin Sessums, Dennis Hensley, Danny Casillas, Ken Slawenski, Rosanne Cash, Pal Shazar, Kathy Valentine, Augusten Burroughs, and Tim Teeman. (Larry Brickman and Mike Rosentreter: You're still with me in my heart.)

Truth be told, this book would have never happened without my agent, Christopher Schelling, who upgraded to being a dear friend during the many years it took me to finally see this dream through. Thanks for your patience and your seemingly endless belief in me.

about the author

Kenneth M. Walsh is a writer, editor, and blogger based in New York City. His popular site—Kenneth in the (212)—has been featured on the *New York Post*'s famed Page Six, Gawker, Romensko, BuzzFeed, *New York* magazine's Daily Intel, Advocate.com, Out.com, and VH1's *Best Week Ever*. In 2012 it was nominated for About.com's Best Gay Blog Readers' Choice award. A graduate of the Walter Cronkite School of Journalism and Mass Communication, Walsh has a career in media that spans two decades, with reporting and editing gigs at the *New York Times,* the *New York Post,* the *Orange County Register,* and the *Arizona Republic.* He is currently a contributor to the Huffington Post and the *Wall Street Journal*'s Speakeasy blog. *Wasn't Tomorrow Wonderful* is his first book.

CPSIA information can be obtained at www.ICGtesting.com
Printed in the USA
LVOW11s1930090314

376635LV00001B/354/P